Colourful
Freezer
Cookery

Colourful
Freezer
Cookery

Edited by Isabelle Barrett

TREASURE PRESS

Notes
* Indicates good bulk cooking.

Plain/all-purpose flour and granulated sugar are used unless otherwise stated.

All spoon measures are level.

Follow only one column of measures.
They are not interchangeable.

Australian Users
All measures in this book are given in metric, imperial and American. Australian users should remember that their tablespoon has been converted to 20 ml, which is larger than the tablespoon used in all columns in this book and, therefore, they should use 3 × 5 ml spoons where instructed to use 1 × 15 ml spoon or 1 tablespoon. If Australian users do not follow the metric column they should also remember that the imperial and Australian pint is 20 fl oz, whereas the American pint is 16 fl oz.

CONTENTS

First published by Octopus Books Ltd
This edition published by Treasure Press
59 Grosvenor Street
London W1

© 1978 Octopus Books Ltd

Reprinted 1983

ISBN 0 907407 48 X

Printed in Hong Kong

INTRODUCTION

The idea of preserving food for long periods of time by making it very cold is not a new one. The Eskimos, who were peculiarly well placed by geography to appreciate the benefits of cold, often stored their food by burying it under the ice. But while this method did prolong life to some extent, it was impossible to use in those very places where food ran the most risk of turning rancid quickly. A technique was needed which enabled food to be kept cold, and therefore fresh, whatever the environment. It was not until the beginning of this century that the problem was solved, with the invention of commercial freezing plants in the United States. This was closely followed by the production of household refrigerators and then, within the last twenty years or so, by home freezing equipment. The result has been not only a revolution in technology but also in the everyday eating and buying habits of millions of ordinary people.

A home freezer will enable you to freeze either cooked or uncooked food from roughly room temperature to a temperature that is cold enough to stop the growth of bacteria and therefore retard or stop the process of deterioration ($-18°C$ or $0°F$). It will also be efficient enough to allow you to insert food into the freezer at room temperature (although only in predetermined quantities), without raising the temperature of the freezer as a whole and therefore altering the temperature of the food it already contains. An officially recognized home freezer is identified in Great Britain by a special symbol (a six-pointed star followed by three smaller stars) to distinguish it from the freezing compartment of a household refrigerator, which is not capable of freezing food in the same way.

The freezing compartment of the refrigerator is merely a conservator of food and should be used only for temporary storage of already frozen food; you should not attempt to use it for freezing cooked or uncooked food from fresh. Conservators will keep food for varying lengths of time, although none of them will store even frozen food for anything like the period of time permitted in a home freezer. Manufacturers' instructions will provide guidelines, but in Great Britain there is a standard symbol to guide you: one star means frozen food can be stored for up to one week, two stars means that the food can be stored for up to one month, while three stars indicates that food can be kept for up to three months. There are no similar standardized symbols in North America, for either home freezers or the conservation compartments of refrigerators.

Types of freezers

There is a wide variety of freezers on the market today. They can be divided into roughly three main types: chest-type freezers, upright freezers and combination refrigerator/freezers.

Chest freezer: this probably has potentially the largest capacity of all the various types on the market, although it does come in different sizes. It is particularly useful to store awkwardly shaped packages and it is also generally considered to be marginally more economical to run than equivalent sizes of other types

Chest freezer

of freezers. Potential disadvantages are that it takes up more floor space than other models and therefore can be difficult to fit into the average kitchen. However, it can be housed elsewhere if you have extra unused space, perhaps in your garage or under the stairs, but it is unwise to put it too far away from the kitchen.

If you are small in terms of height, you should also make absolutely sure that you can reach all the way to the bottom of the freezer without having to be too acrobatic – it is no joke when it comes to cleaning if you have to do a balancing act to get to the lower regions. The greatest single disadvantage of a chest

Refrigerator/freezer

slightly higher running cost (unlike the chest freezer, when you open the door of an upright model, the warm air will penetrate quite far into the interior of the freezer so the freezing mechanism will have to work that much harder to keep the temperature constant), and a slightly more frequent rate of defrosting because of this. If, however, you learn to use the freezer only when you have to, to cut down opening and shutting of the door to an absolute minimum, then operating costs need not mount up.

Refrigerator/freezer: this is probably the most economical of the three main types in terms of space, since it consists of a refrigerator and freezer, either placed on top of each other, or side by side. The main advantage is that the refrigerator plays an important part in the cooling or chilling of food to be home frozen, and it is therefore very useful to have it so near at hand to the freezer. The main disadvantage is that the amount of actual freezer space is rather limited, and for that reason it is probably not the most useful type for the freezer owner with a large family, or one who entertains a great deal.

Maintaining your freezer

When you are buying your freezer, make sure that both the manufacturer and the shop from which you are buying it are reputable and that they maintain both a fast, professional maintenance service and a good supply of spare parts. It often pays to shop around.

Before you first use your freezer and after defrosting, you must always wash it out before starting to pack it with food—follow the manufacturer's instructions explicitly on this where given. A general method recommended is to make a solution of about 1 × 15 ml spoon/1 tablespoon of bicarbonate of soda (baking soda) to about 1.2 litres/2 pints/5 cups of lukewarm water, and gently but thoroughly wash out the interior. Then rinse out with clean water and wipe dry. When using your freezer for the first time, leave it for at least 12 hours before you fill up, and when you do start to stock up initially, take care that you do not exceed the manufacturer's advised ratio of fresh food to be frozen to already frozen food.

Using your freezer

So you are now the owner of a freezer, be it a huge chest-type, a middling upright, or the smallest cube on the market. Regardless of the type you have chosen, the initial investment has been a heavy one, and you are probably anxious to start recouping your outlay – especially if your argument for having a freezer in the first place was that it would not only enable the family to eat better quality meals but save it lots of money as well!

If your freezer is to work for you – and not become an expensive and rather useless luxury – you must use it in the most comprehensive way possible. This means a lot of forward planning on your part, a clear record of what exactly the freezer contains at all times, and stocking it with the widest mixture of food, uncooked, partly cooked, commercially frozen and home-cooked, that you know you will have use for.

Every family varies in its needs, and likes and dislikes, but there are some general basic items that you should at least consider having in your freezer, and there are others which you might do well to avoid for one reason or another.

freezer is probably the comparative inaccessibility of packages on the bottom layers. To operate this type of freezer successfully, you simply have to be organized enough to keep an accurate and up-to-date freezer record, detailing not only what you have, but exactly where it is stored.

Upright freezer: this is probably the easiest type to use, since all the packages are reasonably accessible, and it also takes up far less floor space than a chest-type freezer. Most models, in fact, closely resemble refrigerators in design and take up about the same amount of floor space. Potential disadvantages are a

Meats: you can obtain whole or half carcasses from some butchers who specialize in supplying meat for the freezer, but do consider before you invest in one, whether you would be likely to eat all the parts you will be given (such as belly of pork or breast of lamb) – it could be a false economy if your family's taste runs to roasts and grills (broils). Some butchers, and many freezer centres, offer large packs of mixed meats to suit customers' needs, and these are probably a much better buy for all but the most dedicated meat eaters. Always have a few chops and/or steaks in the freezer, individually packed, and always remember to buy (or pack) stewing beef or minced (ground) meat in usable quantities. Unstuffed, frozen poultry also makes a good standby, as do individual packs of chicken pieces. Most pet food manufacturers also provide frozen meat packs and it might be worth while, if you are a pet owner, to store one or two of these for emergencies.

Vegetables: if you have a vegetable garden, a freezer is practically a necessity for you. Just pick when the vegetables are at their best, blanch according to the individual instructions given on page 16, and pop into the freezer. Even if you do not have a vegetable garden, it is always a good idea to buy vegetables, such as courgettes (zucchini) or broccoli, when they are at their cheapest and freeze, for although they are technically available most of the year round, they do become very expensive and rather a luxury item out of their normal season.

When buying commercially frozen vegetables, buy in free-flow packs so that you can use the quantity you want and return the rest to the freezer.

On the whole, it is not a good idea to clutter up your freezer with vegetables such as potatoes and carrots which are available fresh all year round, unless you want to store an emergency supply.

Fish: almost every type of fish or shellfish can be frozen, and most are available in commercially frozen packs. To home freeze uncooked fish or shellfish yourself, you must be very sure that it is fresh (preferably caught that day). If you have a young family, it is probably mandatory to have at least one large pack of frozen fish fingers in the freezer at any given time!

Fruit: many favourite fruits have very short seasons – strawberries and raspberries, for example – so the only way of enjoying them on anything like a year-round basis is to freeze them when they are plentiful, or to buy them in commercially frozen packs. Many fruits, like vegetables, are sold in free-flow packs by commercial companies and they can therefore be used according to your needs and restocked. For individual instructions on how to pack home-frozen fruit, see the instructions given in the chart on page 21.

Fresh fruit juice (particularly orange and grape-fruit) is sold in frozen concentrated form and makes an excellent 'instant' drink – and is much better for children than sugar-filled fruit squashes and lemonades.

Bakery items: shortcrust pastry (basic pie dough) and puff pastry are available in different-sized blocks ready for thawing and, if you are fond of pies and flans, these are probably an essential for your freezer. Pizzas also freeze very successfully and can be frozen either with the filling already on, or with the filling to be added before cooking. Breads and bread doughs, Danish pastries, sponge cakes and biscuits (cookies) all freeze well and it is probably worth having a stock

of all these items, especially if you entertain regularly.

Dairy produce: ice creams are probably the most popular dairy products to be kept in the freezer, but prepared frozen desserts such as mousses and some commercial yogurts could also be stored away for emergencies. If you wish to keep some cream for emergencies, avoid single (light) cream and stick to double (heavy) or clotted cream, or any type of cream containing more than 40% of butterfat.

Cooked dishes: one of the joys of having a freezer is that you can cut down on the amount of time you spend cooking, or at least concentrate it into a spare afternoon or morning, rather than preparing and cooking every night. Many of the recipes in this book have been 'starred' to indicate that they are particularly suitable for bulk cooking. These recipes can be doubled or trebled in quantity and the proportion you do not want to use immediately can be stored away and frozen for the future. For example, making the filling for cannelloni on page 62 in double or even quadruple quantities and freezing the extra for a future spaghetti sauce can save a lot of precious time and energy.

Cooked food does not keep as long as uncooked food, although the time does vary depending on the ingredients in the dish involved – and to help as a general guideline on this, individual storage times are given after the recipes which follow. You should always plan on saving at least a quarter to a third of your freezer space for cooked dishes.

Useful standbys: a plentiful supply of ice cubes is one of the side benefits of possessing a freezer. An additional stock of already-frozen cubes can be kept in a polythene (plastic) bag to free your ice-cube trays. Stocks can also be stored in ice-cube trays, by boiling them down to concentrate their flavour (see the recipes for beef and chicken stocks on page 33). Concentrated orange juice can be frozen into cubes, then diluted to taste. Some fresh herbs freeze well and a supply of fresh mint, parsley, basil and tarragon, for example, can be obtained by washing, drying and chopping them, then packing into ice-cube trays. Fill the trays with enough water to cover the herbs and then freeze.

When cooking (baking) apples and tomatoes are cheap and plentiful, they can be cooked, puréed and stored in the freezer for later use in sauces, desserts and casseroles.

Open freeze slices of lemon or orange, then put into bags for instant additions to drinks. Grated lemon or orange rind, grated cheese and fresh breadcrumbs also make useful standbys, packed into small tubs or bags.

Baby foods: if you have small children or a baby, then the freezer can really make short work of preparing their food. Purée small portions of any not-too-highly-spiced adult meals you prepare, pack them into yogurt or cream cartons and freeze. Homemade soups and stocks can be thickened with a little mashed potato or baby cereal and packed away in small quantities, and puréed fruit makes a healthy dessert. These are all much cheaper and much tastier than canned baby foods.

The unfreezables: while most foods freeze quite well, there are a few which are not suitable and should therefore be avoided. Salad greens, for instance, go limp. Eggs in their shells should not be frozen because the liquid will expand and break the shell. They can

Useful packaging materials

be frozen, however, if they are shelled and then beaten and packed, about six to a rigid container, with 1×2.5 ml spoon/$\frac{1}{2}$ teaspoon of salt or sugar. Hard-boiled (hard-cooked) eggs discolour, as do avocado pears. Cream and cream cheese containing less than 40% of butterfat should not be frozen, and that includes single (light) cream and most home-made yogurts. Mayonnaise curdles and separates and spaghetti becomes mushy. Other types of pasta, such as lasagne and cannelloni, can be frozen successfully.

Packing for the freezer
One of the most important single steps towards ensuring successful freezing of any dish, whether cooked or uncooked, is to pack it properly. Successful packing means that the food will remain in prime condition during freezing, and will not develop freezer

burn (greyish patches on the surface of the food) or any other effects caused by dehydration. It also ensures that it will not become contaminated during the thawing process and prevents strongly flavoured foods, both cooked and uncooked (garlic-flavoured pâtés or raw chopped onions, for instance) from cross-flavouring other more delicately flavoured foods.

Technically, almost any packaging material is suitable for freezer use if it is moisture- and vapour-proof and crack-proof (i.e. it will prevent loss of natural moisture and juices in the frozen food and withstand temperatures of extreme cold without cracking or breaking). You can test to see if something is crack-proof by half filling it with water, wrapping it in a polythene (plastic) bag and putting it through a dummy run in the freezer – if it does crack, you know to avoid similar containers in the future; if it does not, then it can be added to your supply of freezing equipment.

Most freezer owners, however, rely primarily on what is a huge and bewildering range of commercial packaging materials which have been produced specially for freezer use. These materials can be broken down into roughly three main types:

Sheet wrapping materials: these include heavy-duty aluminium (aluminum) foil, polythene (plastic) wrap and moisture- and vapour-proof paper. Aluminium foil is used primarily for: 1) wrapping large joints of meat or protruding bones on meat and poultry, 2) wrapping bread and cakes, 3) giving extra protection to some foods to be stored in polythene (plastic) bags, 4) in double thickness as a lid or cover to containers without one, and 5) lining casseroles or other dishes. Polythene (plastic) wrap or film and moisture- and vapour-proof paper are used mainly to interleave items such as chops, steaks or hamburgers, to make them suitable for individual use.

Bags: these include polythene (plastic) bags, boil-in-bags, or foil bags. Polythene (plastic) bags are probably the single most popular method of packaging for the freezer, and can be used again and again, providing they remain untainted and unbroken. Just wash in warm soapy water, rinse and turn inside out to dry between uses. Use only heavy-gauge polythene (plastic) for freezing.

Boil-in-bags are similar to polythene (plastic) bags, although they can also be made from foil. They are specially treated so that they can be plunged straight from the freezer into boiling water to thaw and reheat. They are rather more expensive than ordinary polythene (plastic) bags, but make an excellent standby for occasional use. Foil bags are also fairly expensive and, unless you are extremely careful, can only be used once. They are primarily used to store soups and other liquids.

Rigid containers: these include aluminium foil, waxed, polythene (plastic), and toughened glass. Foil or waxed containers come in many shapes and sizes – from pie plates and dishes to pudding basins (oven-proof bowls) and casserole dishes. Many are already fitted with snap-on or other lids, but if not, one can be fashioned from a double thickness of heavy-duty foil. Foil and polythene containers can be used again and again, providing they remain untainted, and should be washed thoroughly in warm soapy water between uses.

If using waxed containers, make sure the food to be stored in them is completely cool before you place it in the container, otherwise the wax will melt. Wax containers can be used more than once but washing shortens their life, since it will affect the wax lining. To ensure a long life, use them as a freezing mould, rather than as a container, by lining with a polythene (plastic) bag then freezing the food and removing the bag from the container when it is frozen. Rigid containers can be used for practically everything, especially soups and prepared dishes of any kind.

'Toughened glass' means glass containers that will not crack under very low temperature conditions; some casserole dishes will qualify, although you may think it rather a waste to immobilize them in the freezer. You can, however, use them in the same way as wax containers above, just shape by lining the dish with a polythene (plastic) bag then remove the bag from the dish when the food is frozen.

Useful standbys: in addition to commercially prepared freezer packaging, most kitchens contain useful standbys. Bottles with wide necks, such as large instant coffee, honey or jam jars make excellent freezing containers, but always remember to do a test run on a new type to make sure that it will withstand the drop in temperature. Screw-top covers form freezer-proof seals, but otherwise seal with heavy-duty foil and freezer tape.

Plastic cartons such as yogurt or cream or margarine tubs can be re-used for freezing small quantities of items such as grated cheese, breadcrumbs and baby foods. If you are storing baby foods in them, always sterilize before using. Snap-on lids make adequate freezer covering, but otherwise use foil and seal with freezer tape.

Ice-cube trays come into their own too, and ensure an adequate supply of ice, stocks and concentrated fruit juices. They are also excellent for freezing herbs.

Sealing and wrapping: in the case of those packaging materials not provided with their own covers, other forms of sealing must be used. The most important thing to remember is that the item being frozen must be absolutely and completely enclosed.

It is vitally important to expel all the air from a polythene (plastic) bag, otherwise the food being frozen will discolour and the freezing process will be slowed down. To expel the air, press gently, starting at the bottom, to force the air up and out; twist the neck firmly, and seal with a twist tie or fold over the top and seal with freezer tape. Another method is to loosely tie the bag, insert a straw or hand vacuum freezer pump and suck out the air, then tighten the fastener and seal with tape.

There are two main methods of wrapping packages for the freezer, one is called 'butcher's wrap', the other 'druggist's wrap'. Both are effective and fairly simple to do. For butcher's wrap, put the food in one corner of the foil or other wrapping material and fold the material up and over the food. Fold in the left and right hand corners, up and over, then bring over the corner opposite. Seal with freezer tape. For druggist's wrap, place the food in the centre of a large piece of wrapping material (it should be large enough to cover the food plus about 10 cm/4 inch overlap). Bring the longest edges over the food, then fold the edges over and over and down towards the food until the edges are tight against it. Fold over the other ends and seal with freezer tape.

Freezer tape, a thick adhesive tape, remains unaffected by frost and is the most commonly used sealing device in freezing. You can, however, seal polythene (plastic) bags and film wrappings by heat-sealing with a special sealing iron or a cool domestic iron. If you are using a domestic iron, however, protect the wrapping material from direct heat with a strip of brown paper.

Labels and records: it is absolutely imperative to keep a clear and up-to-date record of exactly what you have stored, in order to identify the frozen packages when you need them. So the first thing to do is to plan an adequate labelling system, which will give you all the information you need to have about each package in your freezer: the name of the dish or type of food, the quantity or number of servings, and the date on which the food was frozen. It is also a good idea to include the approximate storage life of the food or dish, as a quick reference.

Blanching and packaging Brussels sprouts for the freezer.

Many people find it useful to settle on some sort of colour coding to separate different types of food at a glance, and you can do this quite easily by buying a selection of different-coloured polythene (plastic) bags, and/or different-coloured labels. Then choose an appropriate code which suits your needs, for example, green for vegetables, red for meat and black for cooked food. Chinagraph pencils will write directly onto almost anything, including polythene (plastic) bags, and have the added advantage that they can be washed off when you wish to re-use the containers for something else.

Keeping a separate record book may seem a lot of extra work, but it can be an invaluable guide to exactly what you have stored in the freezer. It can also ensure that cooked dishes are used in proper rotation, thus making sure that everything gets eaten up as and when it should. It also enables you to gauge accurately just what and how much you need of any given type of food at any particular time. You can buy special freezer record books, but it is a simple matter to divide up any child's exercise book into the sections you require: the type of food, the quantity/number of portions, the date on which it was frozen, the storage life and where it is stored in the freezer. But don't forget to cross things off as you use them!

General preparing techniques for the freezer

Since foods themselves are so varied, the methods of preparation for the freezer most suited to individual types of food also vary considerably. There are, however, a few general guidelines common to all successful freezer preparation.

Quality: always use top-quality produce. Freezing does not improve the quality of food, at best it maintains it, and it certainly is not capable of turning an over-ripe, squashy vegetable into a firm just-right item of food. If you plan to grow your own produce specially for freezing, then you would be well advised to plant the special varieties of fruits and vegetables recommended for freezing – most gardening or seed catalogues list these, or your nearest gardening centre could help you identify them.

Speed and hygiene: the sooner you accomplish the transition from fresh to frozen, the more successful you will be with your finished freezer product. The ideal is probably a pick-to-freezer time of about 2 hours, but if there has to be a longer space of time between buying or picking and freezing, chill in the refrigerator until you can complete the preparation. In the case of cooked food, either set aside to cool completely in the refrigerator or put, in the container, into a bowl of crushed ice. The more hygienic your working conditions, the less chance there is of contaminating or cross-flavouring foods, so always make sure that all tools used during preparation, cooking and packaging are scrupulously clean.

In addition to these general guidelines, applicable to some extent to everything you freeze, there are individual techniques you will need to know about.

Fast freezing: it is important to freeze fresh food as rapidly as possible – this method enables you to do this, as well as to freeze cooked and fresh food to the solid state without raising the temperature of the freezer in general, and therefore risking contamination of the already frozen food. In most chest-type freezers there is a special fast freezing compartment, which will enable you to separate the unfrozen food from the frozen. Some upright models, while they do not have a fast freezing compartment, do have a special fast freezing shelf and this can be used to the same purpose. If your freezer does not have a fast freezing compartment or shelf, you can create one for yourself simply by reserving the bottom shelf solely for that purpose.

To fast freeze food, set the switch control a few hours before you intend to fast freeze; the manufacturer's instructions will give you an explicit guide to times. Do not forget to return the switch to its normal position when the food has been solid frozen – usually 12 to 24 hours after the food has been put in. Technically, fast freezing is probably not absolutely necessary for fairly small quantities of food, but do remember that the whole point of freezing is that the quality, flavour and texture of the food being frozen remains as much like fresh as possible. Food which is allowed to reduce to the frozen state relatively slowly will have more time to deteriorate, and will lose some of its nutrients and flavour when it is thawed. As a rule of thumb, if you are freezing small quantities of food which are already very cold (that is, chilled in the refrigerator and/or in a bowl of crushed ice) which are less than 300 ml/½ pint/1¼ cups of liquid, or about 0.5 kg/1 lb of solid food, then it probably is not absolutely necessary. In all other cases, it is much

safer to fast freeze. There are no other special requirements for the process, just pack the food in the materials suggested in individual recipes, or in the guides that follow, and place in the fast freeze compartment or shelf. The length of time an item will take to fast freeze obviously depends very much on the type of food being frozen, the amount and also to some extent on the type of freezer you have.

It is wise not to overload your freezer with fast-freezing food at any one time, and each type of freezer has its recommended fast freeze 'capacity' per 24 hours, this varies from freezer to freezer, so check the manufacturer's instructions for your specific capacity. On average, it is usually about 10% of the complete load capacity.

Open freezing: this is the technique most suitable for more delicate foods, such as decorated cakes, small biscuits (cookies) and cakes, and vegetables and fruits which you wish to pack away in free-flow packs. The process is a simple one: put the food to be open frozen (for example, strawberries or Brussels sprouts) on baking sheets lined with foil and put into the fast freezing compartment until they are solid. The individual fruits and vegetables should be packed fairly tightly together on the baking sheet, but take care that they do not touch each other – otherwise they will freeze that way. When they are frozen, simply pack in polythene (plastic) bags. Again, the time required to freeze to a solid state will vary quite widely depending on the food in question.

Blanching: this is the method reserved almost exclusively for vegetables. It increases the storage time of vegetables dramatically and most, when blanched, will keep for between 9 months and a year (unless otherwise specified in the vegetable freezing chart which follows on page 16).

You can, if you wish, buy special freezer blanching equipment, but you will probably find something in the kitchen which can be used as a blanching basket, such as a fine wire deep frying basket or a French salad basket. Wash and prepare the vegetables according to their specific needs and put them, in small quantities, into the blanching basket. Fast boil a large saucepan half full of water, then plunge the basket into the pan. Completely immerse the vegetables in the fast boiling water, cover the pan and start calculating the blanching time from the minute the water returns to the boil. During the blanching process, gently shake the basket once or twice to make sure the vegetables blanch evenly. Immediately the specified blanching time has been reached, quickly transfer the basket with the vegetables into a bowl of iced water to cool quickly – and keep plenty of extra ice cubes ready to be added to the bowl as the ice melts. On the whole, the vegetables should be cooled in this way for about the same length of time as they were blanched, to ensure that the cooking process has been completely halted. Either open freeze (as above) and put in polythene (plastic) bags when frozen, or pack into rigid containers in usable quantities. The blanching water, incidentally, can be used for about six batches of vegetables. Specific types of vegetables require to be blanched for different lengths of time, and these are given individually in the vegetable freezing chart which follows on page 16.

Fruit syrups and dry sugar packs: both these methods are used exclusively for preparing different types of fruit for the freezer. Fruit syrups are used primarily for fruits which discolour easily and have little natural juice, and can be made up more or less according to your own taste in various strengths or sweetness. There are three standard strengths: for a heavy syrup (45%) about 0.5 kg/1 lb/2 cups of sugar is added per 600 ml/1 pint/2½ cups of water, for a medium syrup (30%) about 225 g/8 oz/1 cup of sugar is added to every 600 ml/1 pint/2½ cups of water. Occasionally when you are dealing with a particularly delicate fruit, a weak (20%) syrup is called for, about 100 g/4 oz/½ cup of sugar per 600 ml/1 pint/2½ cups of water. The best type of syrup for individual fruits is given in the fruit freezing chart which follows on page 21.

Some easily discoloured fruits, such as peaches and apricots will require, in addition to a syrup, a small amount of ascorbic acid (vitamin C), which should be added in order to retain their natural colour. The fruit can either be dipped into a solution of acid and water before packing or the acid can be added to the cold syrup in which the fruit is packed. The usual amount is 0.5 × 2.5 ml spoon/¼ teaspoon of ascorbic acid per 600 ml/1 pint/2½ cups of water or syrup. If you prefer, lemon juice, which contains both ascorbic acid and citric acid, can be used instead, although the quantity needed to be effective (about the juice of 1 lemon to

13

every 900 ml/1½ pints/3¾ cups of water or cold syrup) will affect the taste of the syrup and therefore ultimately the fruit.

To make the syrups, dissolve the sugar in the water, stirring constantly until it has completely disappeared. Boil for about 5 minutes, without stirring, or until the liquid has thickened slightly, then set aside to cool quickly. Always make sure the liquid is cold before you pour it over the food to be frozen. To pack the fruit in the syrup, arrange in slices, halves or chopped in a rigid container and pour over enough syrup to cover the top layer. Usually it is best to leave at least 1 cm/½ inch headspace to allow for expansion during freezing, but individual requirements are given in the fruit freezing chart. Obviously the amount of syrup required per pound of fruit will vary considerably, depending on the preparation, method and type of container being used, but a rough guide when preparing the syrup is to allow about 300 ml/½ pint/1¼ cups per 0.5 kg/1 lb of the fruit to be frozen.

Dry sugar packs are used for those fruits which contain a good deal of natural moisture and the idea is that, on thawing, the sugar sprinkled over and around the fruit will mingle with the juices of the thawing fruit and create a natural syrup. Again, the amount of sugar you use depends a great deal on personal taste, but a good guide would be to use about 0.5 kg/1 lb/ 2 cups of sugar per 2 kg/4½ lb of fruit, and then adjust it up or down according to taste.

To pack fruit in a dry sugar pack, merely arrange it, prepared according to your wish (sliced, chopped, halved, etc.) in layers in a rigid container, sprinkling over a layer of sugar between each layer of fruit. Allow about a 1 cm/½ inch headspace on top, or follow individual requirements listed in the fruit freezing chart. Although granulated sugar can be used for dry sugar packs, caster (superfine) gives better results since it melts more quickly when thawing. The types of fruit best suited to dry sugar packs are detailed in the fruit freezing chart which follows on page 21. Both methods of freezing fruit described above will allow the fruit to be stored in the freezer for up to 1 year, unless otherwise stated in the freezing chart.

Preparing basic foods for the freezer

Meat and poultry: make sure, especially in the case of game, that the meat to be frozen has already been hung for the time necessary to ensure the correct flavour. Always cut large pieces into usable quantities, such as joints (cuts), chops and steaks, if this has not already been done. Fatty meats like minced (ground) beef or pork, should be trimmed of as much excess fat as possible before packing. Kidneys should be cored and liver trimmed of gristle and membrane. Poultry can be frozen whole, or in serving portions. If you are freezing whole, try to make the bird as compact as possible and especially try to get rid of any protruding bones which might puncture the wrapping material. If you are unable to do this, wrap the bones with foil before packing. Never stuff poultry before freezing since stuffings, on the whole, have a much shorter freezer life than uncooked meat. Pack larger quantities of meat, such as joints (cuts) and whole poultry or game, either by wrapping in heavy-duty foil and/or putting in polythene (plastic) bags and sealing with freezer tape. Cubed meat for stewing and minced (ground) meat should be stored, in usable quantities, in polythene (plastic) bags and sealed with freezer

tape. Interleave individual chops, steaks and liver slices with heavy-duty foil or freezer film, and either wrap in heavy-duty foil or put in polythene (plastic) bags and seal tightly with freezer tape. Individual storage times for different types of meat are given in the general storage chart which follows on page 28.

Fish: only freshly caught fish, or fish caught the same day, should be home frozen, and then as quickly as possible. Scale, gut and trim fins, etc. from whole fish before freezing (the head and tail can either be left on or removed, according to taste). Wrap securely in foil, then seal with freezer tape. Freeze only one large whole fish at a time in the fast freeze compartment. Pack fillets and steaks in separate portions by interleaving with foil or film before overwrapping. Crab and lobster should be cooked before freezing. Pack whole in heavy-duty foil or polythene (plastic) bags, or remove the meat from the shells and pack into small rigid containers. Large prawns (shrimp) are best frozen with the head, legs and claws removed. Small shrimps can either be frozen raw, or may be simmered until they become pink, then cooled in the cooking water before being drained and packed into cartons or other rigid containers.

Dairy produce: you will probably want to store most dairy products in only 'emergency' portions since they remain fairly stable in price and are available all the year round. Butter, margarine and other fats need only to be overwrapped, either in heavy-duty foil or in a polythene (plastic) bag and sealed with freezer tape, to be stored successfully.

Although eggs cannot be stored whole, you can shell them and store the yolk and white beaten together (about six to a rigid container to which a pinch of salt or sugar has been added), or they may also be stored separately. The whites should be beaten until they are frothy with a little salt or sugar and packed into rigid containers or ice-cube trays. Thaw and use in the usual way. Egg yolks can be beaten and stored in the same way. Always remember to mark whether you have stored the egg with salt or sugar on the label, as it could be an unpleasant shock to find you have sugar-tasting eggs in a savoury dish.

Ice cream can usually be stored in the container in which it was bought. Creams, as discussed earlier, should not be frozen unless they have a butterfat content of 40%, which means that all single (light) creams are unsatisfactory, and some whipping creams too. Double (heavy) cream can separate sometimes and for best results, should be chilled, whipped and transferred into small cartons.

Cakes and pastries: most cakes and pastries freeze very well, both cooked and uncooked. Pastry, for instance, can be made up in large quantities and frozen in usable amounts. To freeze, wrap in a polythene (plastic) bag or foil and seal with freezer tape. Baked or unbaked flan cases (pie shells) can be open frozen then stacked on top of each other (interleaved with foil or film) before being overwrapped in polythene (plastic) bags for extra protection. Homemade breads and rolls should be packed, when cold, in foil then overwrapped in polythene (plastic) bags. Open freeze decorated cakes to preserve their decoration, then pack in polythene (plastic) bags or wrap in foil. Only icings (frostings) containing a proportion of fat will freeze satisfactorily, so avoid cakes decorated with fondant, water icing or boiled icings. Undecorated cakes such as fruit cakes, can be packed in polythene (plastic) bags or foil, or frozen already sliced, with the slices interleaved with foil or film.

Fruit: fruit can be prepared in one of four ways for the freezer: it can be open frozen, packed in a dry sugar pack or in a syrup pack (see page 13), or puréed, either by cooking and mashing, or simply by mashing uncooked, and frozen in rigid containers, allowing headspace for expansion where necessary.

Open freezing is probably the best method of freezing small fruits such as blackberries, raspberries and strawberries, so that they are free flowing when packed. Dry sugar packs are best suited to fruits with a good deal of natural juice, such as citrus fruits and blackcurrants. Syrup packs are intended primarily for fruits with a low juice content such as apricots and pears. Some tough-skinned fruits, such as gooseberries (especially if they are to be stewed or made into jam) can be packed dry straight into polythene (plastic) bags and frozen. Some other fruits, such as bananas, are really only successfully frozen already puréed, and of course any fruit which is intended primarily as a flavouring for mousses or fools is, for convenience, best puréed before freezing. For the best freezing methods suited to individual fruits, see the fruit freezing chart which follows on page 21.

Vegetables: if you are storing vegetables for only a very short time (up to about 6 weeks) then you can open freeze them uncooked (unblanched), or pack into rigid containers and block freeze. If, however, you wish to store them for a greater length of time,

then in almost every case the vegetable must be blanched before being frozen. Individual blanching times vary according to the vegetable in question and are given in the vegetable freezing chart which follows on page 16. They should be adhered to very precisely for successful freezing results. After blanching the vegetables can be open frozen then packed in polythene (plastic) bags, or they may be stored in rigid containers, in usable quantities. Remember that blanching is a cooking process and therefore, when the vegetable is to be cooked after freezing, the amount of cooking time required will be less.

It is always essential to know not only exactly what is in your freezer, but when it was put there, and how long it can be kept in prime condition. For even frozen food begins to deteriorate eventually, and that can mean anything from about 1 week to 1 year, depending on the type of food in question. The guide which follows is an approximate one, but exceeding it could mean that you will be left with food which has deteriorated to some extent in not only flavour and texture but also appearance. The times given below apply both to home-frozen food and commercially prepared food. Commercial manufacturers freeze their produce at temperatures well below the capabilities of even the most advanced and sophisticated home freezer, so that the enzymes in the food remain inactive for much longer than they would in the same food home frozen.

Illustrated below are some of the many ways in which pastry can be frozen.

Vegetable Freezing Chart

VEGETABLE/PREPARATION	BLANCHING TIME	PACKAGING	COOKING
Artichokes, globe. Remove the outer leaves and stalk. Trim tops and wash well. Add a little lemon juice to the blanching water.	Medium – 7–10 minutes	Pack in rigid containers, leaving about 1 cm/½ inch headspace, or in polythene (plastic) bags.	Plunge frozen into boiling salted water for 5 minutes.
Artichokes, Jerusalem. Scrub, peel, then cook in boiling water until tender (about 30–40 minutes). Push through a strainer or purée in a blender.	Nil	Spoon the purée into rigid containers, leaving about 2.5 cm/1 inch headspace. Recommended storage time: not more than 3 months.	Reheat gently from frozen with a little milk or butter, or add frozen to soups.
Asparagus. Trim the stalks to even lengths, then scrape the lower part. Separate into bundles according to the thickness of the stalk. After blanching tie in 100 g/4 oz bundles.	Thick stalks – 4 minutes Thin stalks – 2 minutes	Pack in rigid containers, alternating bundles tip to tail.	Plunge frozen into boiling salted water for 5–8 minutes.
Aubergine (eggplant). Peel and cut into thin slices. Either use a stainless steel knife for this or sprinkle over lemon juice to avoid discoloration.	4 minutes	Open freeze for free-flow packs, or pack in polythene (plastic) bags or in rigid containers, leaving about 1 cm/½ inch headspace.	Plunge frozen into boiling salted water for 5 minutes.
Beans, broad (lima). Choose young beans, shell and grade according to size. Discard any starchy ones.	Medium – 3 minutes Small – 2 minutes	Open freeze for free-flow packs or pack in polythene (plastic) bags or in rigid containers, leaving about 1 cm/½ inch headspace.	Plunge frozen into boiling salted water for 5–8 minutes.
Beans, French (green) and runner (snap). Choose young, stringless beans and top and tail (clean). Leave whole, slice or chop.	Whole – 3 minutes Chopped or sliced – 2 minutes	Open freeze for free-flow packs or pack in polythene (plastic) bags or in rigid containers, leaving about 1 cm/½ inch headspace.	Plunge frozen into boiling salted water for 5–8 minutes.
Beetroot (beets). Select young small beetroot (beets). Trim, leaving about 2.5 cm/1 inch of stem attached. Cook in boiling water until tender (about 30–45 minutes), then cool and rub off the outer skin. Leave whole or slice.	Nil	Pack in rigid containers, leaving 1 cm/½ inch headspace, or in polythene (plastic) bags. Recommended storage time: not more than 6 months.	Thaw in the refrigerator for 2–6 hours before using.
Beets. See *Beetroot*			
Broccoli. Trim, wash in salted water and cut into sprigs. Trim the stalks to even lengths and grade according to thickness of the stalk.	Thick stalks – 3–5 minutes Thin stalks – 2 minutes	Open freeze for free-flow packs, or pack in polythene (plastic) bags, or in rigid containers, leaving about 1 cm/½ inch headspace.	Plunge frozen into boiling salted water for 5–8 minutes.
Brussels sprouts. Choose small sprouts, wash and grade according to size. Trim the outside leaves.	Medium sprouts – 4 minutes Small sprouts – 3 minutes	Open freeze for free-flow packs, or pack in polythene (plastic) bags, or in rigid containers, leaving about 1 cm/½ inch headspace.	Plunge frozen into boiling salted water for 5–8 minutes.

VEGETABLE/PREPARATION	BLANCHING TIME	PACKAGING	COOKING
Cabbage, red and white. Choose firm solid cabbages and trim the outside leaves. Shred or cut into wedges.	Shredded – 1½ minutes Wedges – 4 minutes	Pack in polythene (plastic) bags, or in rigid containers, leaving about 1 cm/½ inch headspace. Recommended storage time: not more than 6 months.	Plunge frozen into boiling salted water for about 5 minutes. Do not use frozen cabbage in salads, such as coleslaw.
Carrots. Choose young small carrots. Scrape and leave small carrots whole, or dice or quarter large ones. Grade according to size.	Whole – 5 minutes Sliced or quartered – 3 minutes	Open freeze for free-flow packs or pack in polythene (plastic) bags, or in rigid containers, leaving about 1 cm/½ inch headspace.	Plunge frozen into boiling salted water for about 5 minutes. Diced or quartered carrots can be added frozen to stews and casseroles.
Cauliflower. Choose creamy, compact heads. Trim and separate into small florets. Add a little lemon juice to the blanching water.	3 minutes	Open freeze for free-flow packs or pack in polythene (plastic) bags. Recommended storage time: not more than 6 months.	Plunge frozen into boiling salted water for 5–8 minutes.
Celeriac. Trim, scrape and cut into thin slices, or chop. Steam until almost tender.	Nil	Open freeze for free-flow packs or pack in polythene (plastic) bags. Recommended storage time: not more than 9 months.	Plunge frozen into boiling salted water for 8 minutes. Or add chopped and frozen to casseroles. Use only for cooked dishes.
Celery. Choose young tender stalks. Wash, trim and remove any strings. Cut into small even-sized lengths. Freeze hearts whole.	Hearts – 8 minutes Stalks – 3 minutes	Pack, in usable quantities, in polythene (plastic) bags, or in rigid containers, leaving about 1 cm/½ inch headspace.	Add frozen to stews and casseroles. Use only for cooked dishes.
Chicory (French or Belgian endive). Select fresh white heads. Discard discoloured leaves. Add a little lemon juice to the blanching water.	2 minutes	Pack in polythene (plastic) bags or in rigid containers, leaving about 1 cm/½ inch headspace.	Plunge frozen into boiling salted water, with 1 × 5 ml spoon/1 teaspoon of sugar, for 8 minutes. Do not use frozen chicory in salads.
Corn-on-the-cob. Choose young tender cobs. Remove the outside leaves and silk. Grade according to size.	Medium cobs – 6 minutes Small cobs – 4 minutes	Freeze separately and pack in polythene (plastic) bags. Or remove the kernels and open freeze for free-flow packs.	Thaw whole cobs for 6 hours at room temperature, before plunging into boiling salted water for 8–10 minutes, or plunge frozen kernels into boiling salted water for 5 minutes.
Courgettes (zucchini). Choose small young courgettes (zucchini). Wash and cut in half if very small or into even-sized slices.	1 minute	Open freeze for free-flow packs, or pack into rigid containers, interleaving the layers with foil or film wrap. Allow about 1 cm/½ inch headspace.	Plunge frozen into boiling salted water for 3 minutes, or thaw and sauté in butter.
Eggplant. See *Aubergine*			
Fennel. Choose small compact bulbs. Trim, wash and cut into even-sized pieces.	3 minutes	Pack in usable quantities in polythene (plastic) bags or in rigid containers, leaving about 1 cm/½ inch headspace.	Plunge frozen into boiling salted water for 8 minutes. Or add frozen to stews and casseroles. Do not use frozen fennel in salads.
French or Belgian endive. See *Chicory*			

VEGETABLE/PREPARATION	BLANCHING TIME	PACKAGING	COOKING
Green beans. See *Beans, French*			
Kohlrabi. Choose small young roots. Trim, wash and peel. Leave very small kohlrabi whole, chop larger ones into even-sized pieces.	Whole – 3 minutes Chopped – 1 minute	Open freeze for free-flow packs or pack in polythene (plastic) bags.	Plunge frozen into boiling salted water for 8–12 minutes.
Leeks. Wash thoroughly, trim and remove the outside leaves. Cut into even-sized pieces or leave very small ones whole.	Whole – 4 minutes Chopped – 2 minutes	Pack in polythene (plastic) bags or in rigid containers, leaving about 1 cm/½ inch headspace. Recommended storage time: not more than 6 months.	Plunge frozen into boiling salted water for 8–10 minutes. Or add chopped leeks frozen to stews and casseroles.
Lima beans. See *Beans, broad*			
Marrow (summer squash). Use only young marrow. Trim, peel and remove the seeds. Cut into even-sized pieces.	3 minutes	Pack in polythene (plastic) bags or in rigid containers, leaving about 1 cm/½ inch headspace. Recommended storage time: up to 10 months.	Plunge frozen into boiling salted water for 3–5 minutes.
Mixed vegetables. Prepare each vegetable according to separate needs.	Blanch each separately according to specific instructions	Mix the vegetables, then put in polythene (plastic) bags or in rigid containers, leaving about 1 cm/½ inch headspace.	Plunge frozen into boiling salted water for 3–5 minutes. Or add frozen to stews and casseroles.
Mushrooms. Choose as fresh as possible. Wipe thoroughly and leave whole or slice. Add a little lemon juice to the cooking juice.	Do not blanch but fry gently in butter for 2–3 minutes	Pack in rigid containers, with the cooking juice, leaving about 1 cm/½ inch headspace. Recommended storage time: not more than 3 months.	Reheat gently in the cooking juices. Or add frozen to soups, stews and casseroles.
Onions. Choose very small whole onions, or chop or slice larger ones.	Whole – 2 minutes Sliced – 1 minute	Pack in polythene (plastic) bags and, if storing for some time, put in second bag to prevent any cross-flavouring. Recommended storage time, blanched: not more than 6 months; unblanched: not more than 3 months.	Add frozen to soups, stews and casseroles.
Parsnips. Choose small tender parsnips. Trim and peel. Cut into small even-sized pieces.	2 minutes	Open freeze for free-flow packs, or pack in polythene (plastic) bags, or in rigid containers, leaving about 1 cm/½ inch headspace.	Plunge frozen into boiling salted water for 10–12 minutes.
Peas. Choose young sweet peas. Shell and discard any blemished peas.	1 minute	Open freeze for free-flow packs, or pack in polythene (plastic) bags, or in rigid containers, leaving about 1 cm/½ inch headspace.	Plunge frozen into boiling salted water for 4–7 minutes. Or add frozen to stews and casseroles.
Peas, mange-tout (snow). Choose flat young pods. Top, tail and string (clean).	2–3 minutes	Open freeze for free-flow packs or pack in polythene (plastic) bags, or in rigid containers, leaving about 1 cm/½ inch headspace.	Plunge frozen into boiling salted water for 5–8 minutes.

VEGETABLE/PREPARATION	BLANCHING TIME	PACKAGING	COOKING
Peppers, red or green. Freeze whole with seeds and pith removed for use uncooked. Deseed and chop or slice for use cooked.	Whole – 3 minutes Sliced – 2 minutes	Freeze individually whole and pack in polythene (plastic) bags. Pack chopped or sliced in rigid containers, leaving about 1 cm/½ inch headspace. Recommended storage time: not more than 6 months.	Plunge chopped or sliced into boiling salted water for 5–10 minutes. Thaw whole in refrigerator and stuff or use uncooked.
Potatoes, new. Choose only small potatoes. Scrub and grade according to size.	Small – 5 minutes Very small – 4 minutes	Pack in polythene (plastic) bags with a few mint sprigs. Recommended storage time: not more than 6 months.	Plunge frozen into boiling salted water for 10 minutes.

VEGETABLE/PREPARATION	BLANCHING TIME	PACKAGING	COOKING
Potatoes, boiled. Grade according to size, wash and peel. Boil (add some mint sprigs according to taste), until just slightly undercooked.	Nil	Pack in polythene (plastic) bags or boil-in-bags. Recommended storage time: not more than 3 months.	Plunge frozen into boiling salted water for 3–5 minutes, or put boil-in-bags into boiling water, remove from heat and soak for 10 minutes.
Potatoes, mashed. Cook and mash potatoes in the usual way. Make into croquette or duchesse potatoes.	Nil	Open freeze for free-flow packs, then pack in polythene (plastic) bags. Recommended storage time: not more than 3 months.	Reheat from frozen, depending on whether croquettes or duchesse, or according to recipe.
Potatoes, French-fried. Peel and cut old potatoes into even-sized pieces, or fingers. Deep fry in hot oil until just pale but not brown.	Nil	Open freeze for free-flow packs, then pack in polythene (plastic) bags. Recommended storage time: not more than 6 months.	Shallow fry or deep fry from frozen.
Potatoes, roast. Boil old potatoes until they are nearly cooked. Drain and put in a roasting pan. Roast, with a little oil added, in a preheated moderately hot oven (200°C/400°F, Gas Mark 6) for 1 hour. Cool quickly.	Nil	Pack in polythene (plastic) bags. Recommended storage time: not more than 6 months.	Put frozen potatoes in roasting pan with a little oil added, then roast in a moderately hot oven (190°C/375°F, Gas Mark 5) for 30 minutes.
Rutabaga. See *Swede*			
Snap beans. See *Beans, runner*			
Snow peas. See *Peas, mange-tout*			
Spinach. Choose tender young leaves and wash very thoroughly. Drain out excess moisture. Blanch only small amounts at a time.	2 minutes	Pack in rigid containers, leaving about 1 cm/½ inch headspace, or in polythene (plastic) bags.	Plunge frozen into boiling salted water for 3–5 minutes.
Summer squash. See *Marrow*			
Swede (rutabaga). Trim, peel and cut into small even-sized pieces.	3 minutes	Open freeze for free-flow packs, or pack in polythene (plastic) bags, or in rigid containers, leaving about 1 cm/½ inch headspace.	Plunge frozen into boiling salted water for 8–10 minutes. Or add frozen to stews and casseroles.
Tomatoes. Blanch and skin and leave whole or purée.	Nil	Pack whole skinned tomatoes in polythene bags or rigid containers. Freeze purée in rigid containers, leaving about 1 cm/½ inch headspace.	Thaw in the refrigerator and add to stews, soups, sauces and casseroles. Do not use frozen tomatoes in salads. Use only for cooking.
Turnip. Choose small tender turnips. Trim, peel and cut into small even-sized pieces.	Small, whole – 4 minutes Chopped – 2 minutes	Open freeze for free-flow packs, or pack in polythene (plastic) bags, or in rigid containers, leaving about 1 cm/½ inch headspace.	Plunge frozen into boiling salted water for 10 minutes. Or add chopped pieces frozen to stews, soups and casseroles.
Zucchini. See *Courgettes*			

Fruit Freezing Chart

FRUIT/PREPARATION	PACKAGING	THAWING
Apples. Choose only perfect fruit. Peel, core and slice. Blanch for 1 minute if open freezing.	Soak in ascorbic acid or lemon juice solution (to prevent discoloration), then either dry and open freeze for free-flow packs, or pack in dry sugar or with medium or light syrup in rigid containers, leaving about 1 cm/½ inch headspace.	Thaw, covered, in the refrigerator and either use in pies or flans, or turn frozen into a saucepan and thaw over a very low heat, stirring occasionally, for stewed.
Apples, puréed. Peel, core and chop. Cook in very little water, with or without sugar, until soft. Purée in a blender, or mash with a fork.	Pack into rigid containers, leaving about 1 cm/½ inch headspace. Recommended storage time: not more than 6 months.	Thaw, covered, in the refrigerator, and then use for mousses, fools or sauces.
Apricots. Choose firm but ripe apricots. Blanch, peel and remove the stones (seeds). Either halve or slice. Alternatively, to make a purée, simmer the fruit in very little water, with sugar, until soft. Purée in a blender, or mash with a fork.	Pack with heavy syrup, to which ascorbic acid or lemon juice, has been added, in rigid containers. Fill the headspace with crumpled foil to keep the fruit immersed in the syrup. Pack purée in rigid containers, leaving about 1 cm/½ inch headspace. Recommended storage time for purée: not more than 6 months.	Thaw, covered, for 3 hours at room temperature. Or turn the frozen fruit and syrup into a saucepan and thaw over a very low heat. Thaw purée, covered, in the refrigerator, and add to mousses, fools, flans etc.
Avocado pears. Discolour badly when frozen whole, and therefore best stored as a purée. Remove the stone (seed) and mash the flesh to a purée. Beat in about 1 × 5 ml spoon/ 1 teaspoon of lemon juice to each pulped avocado.	Pack in small rigid containers. Recommended storage time: not more than 3 months.	Thaw, covered, in the refrigerator and use in mousses, dips and pâtés, or add to cold soups.

FRUIT/PREPARATION	PACKAGING	THAWING
Bananas. Discolour badly when frozen whole, and therefore best stored as a purée. Peel and mash the flesh to a purée with a fork, or in a blender. Add 1 × 15 ml spoon/ 1 tablespoon of lemon juice and about 25 g/1 oz/2 tablespoons of sugar to each 0.5 kg/1 lb of purée.	Pack in small rigid containers. Recommended storage time: not more than 3 months.	Thaw, covered, in the refrigerator and use as a sandwich filling, for fools or mousses, or for addition to tea breads.
Blackberries. Choose only firm young berries and discard any woody stalks. Wash only if necessary. Dry well.	Open freeze for free-flow packs, or pack with dry sugar in rigid containers, leaving about 1 cm/ ½ inch headspace. Or pack with medium syrup in rigid containers. Fill the headspace with crumpled foil to keep the fruit immersed in the syrup.	Thaw, covered, in the refrigerator. Serve partially frozen for desserts, or for addition to crumbles and pies. Or turn frozen fruit and syrup into a saucepan and thaw over a very low heat.
Cherries. Choose young, sweet fruit. Preferably freeze red cherries rather than black. Remove the stalks and stones (pits).	Open freeze for free-flow packs or pack with dry sugar in rigid containers, leaving about 1 cm/½ inch headspace. Or pack with medium or heavy syrup in rigid containers. Fill the headspace with crumpled foil to keep the fruit immersed in the syrup.	Thaw, covered, at room temperature or in the refrigerator for pies and fruit salads. Or turn the frozen fruit and syrup into a saucepan and thaw over a very low heat.
Cranberries. Choose only perfect fruit. Remove the stalks. To make a purée, simmer the fruit in very little water, with sugar, until soft. Mash with a fork, or purée in a blender.	Pack with dry sugar in rigid containers, or pack purée in small rigid containers, leaving about 1 cm/½ inch headspace.	Thaw, covered, in the refrigerator. Use whole cranberries for sauces or garnish, and purées for mousses or sauces.
Currants, black, red and white. Choose only perfect fruit. Blackcurrants have the best flavour of the three for freezing. Top and tail (clean) and wash and dry well. To make a purée, simmer in very little water, with sugar, until soft. Mash with a fork or purée in a blender.	Open freeze for free-flow packs or pack with dry sugar in rigid containers. Or pack with light syrup in rigid containers. Fill the headspace with crumpled foil to keep the fruit immersed in the syrup. Pack purées in rigid containers, leaving about 1 cm/ ½ inch headspace.	Thaw, covered, at room temperature for 3 hours for pies and fruit salads. Or turn the frozen fruit and syrup into a saucepan and thaw over a very low heat.

FRUIT/PREPARATION	PACKAGING	THAWING
Damsons. Not really suitable for freezing whole because of their tough skins, and the stones (pits) can flavour the fruit. Simmer chopped fruit in very little water, with sugar, until soft. Mash with a fork or purée in a blender.	Pack in rigid containers, leaving about 1 cm/½ inch headspace.	Thaw, covered, in the refrigerator for addition to fools or mousses, and for jams.
Dates. Leave whole or cut in half and remove stones (pits).	Open freeze whole dates for free-flow packs. Pack halved dates in light syrup in rigid containers.	Thaw, covered, at room temperature.
Figs. Choose only ripe fruit and handle very carefully. Leave whole or blanch and peel.	Pack, unpeeled, in rigid containers. Or pack peeled fruit with medium syrup in rigid containers. Fill the headspace with crumpled foil to keep the fruit immersed in the syrup.	Thaw, covered, in the refrigerator. Use unpeeled in salads or as a dessert with cream. Figs with syrup can be used for pies, flans and mousses.
Gooseberries. Choose only ripe berries. Either top and tail (clean) and leave whole, or simmer in very little water, with sugar, until soft. Mash softened fruit with a fork or purée in a blender.	Open freeze for free-flow packs or pack with dry sugar, or medium syrup, in rigid containers, leaving about 1 cm/½ inch headspace. Pack purées in rigid containers, leaving about 1 cm/½ inch headspace.	Thaw, covered, for 4 hours at room temperature. Use in jams and crumbles. Thawed purée may be added to fools and mousses.
Grapefruit. See *Oranges*		
Grapes. Choose only fruit with delicate skins. Halve and remove the pips (seeds). Seedless varieties can be frozen whole.	Pack both whole and halved with medium syrup in rigid containers, leaving about 1 cm/½ inch headspace.	Thaw, covered, for 2 hours at room temperature. Add to pies and fruit salads.
Greengages. Choose only perfect fruit. Not really suitable for freezing whole because the stones (pits) can flavour the fruit. Halve and remove the stones (pits).	Open freeze for free-flow packs. Or partially fill a rigid container with heavy syrup, add the fruit and cover with more syrup. Fill the headspace with crumpled foil to keep the fruit immersed in the syrup.	Thaw, covered, in the refrigerator and use for pies or crumbles, or for jams.
Lemons. Usually frozen either grated (the rind) or sliced. The juice can also be stored separately. Slice the fruit with rind on and remove any pips (seeds).	Sliced lemons: open freeze for free-flow packs. Grated lemon rind: pack in very small rigid containers. Lemon juice: freeze with or without added sugar, in ice-cube trays, then pack in polythene (plastic) bags.	Thaw at room temperature for 3 hours. Use sliced lemons for drinks or as garnish for savoury dishes. Rind and juice may be added as required in individual recipes.
Loganberries. Choose only firm young berries. Wash, drain and dry. Or simmer, with sugar, until soft and mash with a fork or purée in a blender.	Open freeze for free-flow packs or pack with dry sugar in rigid containers, leaving about 1 cm/½ inch headspace. Pack purée in small quantities in freezer bags or rigid containers.	Thaw, covered, in the refrigerator and add to puddings and sauces.
Melons. Choose only ripe fruit. Peel, halve and remove the seeds. Cut into slices, cubes or scoop into balls.	Pack with dry sugar in rigid containers, leaving about 1 cm/½ inch headspace, or with light syrup in rigid containers. Fill the headspace with crumpled foil to keep the fruit immersed in the syrup.	Thaw, covered, at room temperature for 3 hours. Serve still slightly frosty.

FRUIT/PREPARATION	PACKAGING	THAWING
Oranges. Whole oranges (with the exception of Sevilles) go bitter during freezing. Peel and separate into segments or slice. Remove the pips (seeds). The juice can also be stored separately.	Pack Sevilles whole in polythene (plastic) bags. Pack segments or slices with medium syrup in rigid containers, leaving about 1 cm/½ inch headspace. Freeze juice, with or without added sugar, in ice-cube trays, then pack in polythene (plastic) bags.	Use Sevilles frozen for making marmalades. Thaw other types, covered, for 3 hours at room temperature. Add to fruit salads or serve alone.
Peaches. Choose only perfect fruit. Blanch and peel. Halve or slice and remove the stone (seed).	Pack with heavy syrup, to which ascorbic acid or lemon juice has been added, in rigid containers. Fill the headspace with crumpled foil to keep the fruit immersed in the syrup.	Thaw, covered, at room temperature for 4 hours. Add to fruit salads or pies, or serve chilled with a little brandy sprinkled over.
Pears. Pears do not, on the whole, freeze as well as other fruit so, for best results, choose perfect but slightly under-ripe fruit. Peel, core and cut into slices, or leave halved. Poach in medium syrup for 1½ minutes. Drain and cool.	Pack with medium syrup, to which ascorbic acid or lemon juice has been added, in rigid containers. Fill the headspace with crumpled foil to keep the fruit immersed in the syrup.	Thaw, covered, at room temperature for 4 hours. Add to fruit salads or pies, or poach in red wine. Serve alone with a little white wine or Cointreau sprinkled over.
Pineapples. Choose only firm ripe fruit. Peel and core, then cut into into rings or chunks.	Pack dry with or without sugar in rigid containers, interleaving slices with foil. Or pack with light syrup in rigid containers. Fill the headspace with crumpled foil to keep the fruit immersed in the syrup.	Thaw at room temperature for 3–4 hours. Add partially chilled to fruit salads. Or serve alone with a little kirsch sprinkled over.
Plums. Choose only perfect ripe fruit. Not really suitable for freezing whole because the skin is tough and the stones (pits) can flavour the fruit. Halve and remove the stones (pits).	Pack with medium or heavy syrup in rigid containers. Fill the headspace with crumpled foil to keep the fruit immersed in the syrup. Or pack dry in polythene (plastic) bags, but do not store for longer than 3 months.	Thaw, covered, at room temperature for 3 hours and add to pies and flans. Or turn the frozen fruit and syrup into a saucepan and thaw over a low heat. Use dry pack for jams.
Raspberries. Choose only perfect fruit, and handle sparingly. Leave whole or mash gently to a purée.	Open freeze for free-flow packs, or pack with light syrup in rigid containers, leaving about 1 cm/½ inch headspace. Pack purées in small rigid containers, leaving about 1 cm/½ inch headspace.	Thaw, covered, at room temperature for 3 hours, and add to fruit salads. Or serve alone just before fully thawed. Use purées as a base for ice cream, sauces, fools, mousses, etc.
Rhubarb. Choose only firm, slender stalks with little fibre. Wash and dry. Trim, remove the fibre and cut into even-sized lengths. Blanch in boiling water for 1 minute to retain colour and flavour. Drain and cool.	Open freeze for free-flow packs, or pack with heavy syrup in rigid containers, leaving about 1 cm/½ inch headspace.	Thaw partially at room temperature and add to pies and crumbles, or use for jams. Or turn the frozen fruit and syrup into a saucepan and thaw over a very low heat.
Strawberries. Choose only perfect fruit and handle sparingly. Leave whole if small or halve or slice larger fruit. Mash large soft berries with a fork or purée in a blender.	Open freeze for free-flow packs. Or pack with dry sugar in rigid containers, or with medium syrup in rigid containers, leaving about 1 cm/½ inch headspace. Pack purées in small rigid containers, leaving about 1 cm/½ inch headspace.	Thaw, covered, at room temperature for 3 hours and add to fruit salads. Add to jams and pies, or serve alone slightly frosty. Serve purée as a sauce for ice cream, or add to mousses, fools, etc.

Basic Foods Freezing Chart

FOOD	PACKAGING/PREPARATION	STORAGE TIME
BAKED FOOD		
Bread, sliced	Keep in waxed wrapping, overwrap with foil and seal with freezer tape.	6 months
Bread, crusty	Wrap in foil, then put in polythene (plastic) bag and seal.	1 week
Yeast pastries (Danish, croissants, etc.)	Put in polythene (plastic) bags and seal.	1 month
Sand-wiches	Avoid fillings which do not freeze well. Wrap individually in foil then put in polythene (plastic) bags, or pack in rigid containers, interleaving with foil or film.	1½ months
Unbaked dough, risen	Doughs containing yeast lose their resilience quite quickly. Put in lightly greased polythene (plastic) bags, leaving a little headspace to allow the yeast to rise a little before freezing solid.	3 weeks
Unbaked doughs, unrisen	Pack in lightly greased polythene (plastic) bags, leaving enough space for the dough to double in size.	2 months
Cakes	Open freeze decorated cakes, otherwise pack in polythene (plastic) bags. Pack small cakes in rigid containers, interleaving with foil or film, or open freeze for free-flow packs.	Decorated cakes and gingerbread: 2 months Undecorated: 4 months Fat-free sponges: 10 months
Flans or tarts, baked	Wrap in foil or film, then put in polythene (plastic) bags. Or open freeze then stack flan cases on top of each other, separating the layers with foil or film. Overwrap with foil and seal.	Unfilled: 6 months Filled: 2 months
Flans or tarts, unbaked, unfilled	As for baked above.	3 months

FOOD	PACKAGING/PREPARATION	STORAGE TIME
Scones and biscuits (cookies)	Open freeze for free-flow packs, or pack in rigid containers interleaving with foil or film. Biscuits (cookies) with a high butter content (such as shortbread) will keep for only half the time of most other biscuits (cookies).	6 months
DAIRY PRODUCE		
Butter	Overwrap waxed wrapping with foil and seal.	Unsalted: 6 months Salted: 3 months
Cheese	Wrap cheese in foil and seal. Hard and blue cheeses often become crumbly after freezing.	3–6 months, according to condition and freshness at time of freezing.
Cream	See page 14 for best methods of storing cream. Never freeze single (light) cream or any other type containing less than 40% butterfat.	3 months
Eggs	See page 14 for best method of storing eggs. Never freeze with shells intact.	6 months
Ice cream	Store in bought container. Pack homemade in waxed or rigid containers, leaving about 1 cm/½ inch headspace.	Homemade: 3 months Commercially made: 4–6 weeks
Milk	Only homogenized milk is suitable for freezing. Store in waxed or other rigid containers, leaving about 5 cm/2 inch headspace.	1 month
FISH		
Oil fish (herrings, mackerel, trout, mullet, salmon, etc.)	Usually frozen whole. See page 14 for best methods of preparing for freezing.	3 months
White fish (whiting, sole, cod, plaice (flounder), etc.)	Usually frozen filleted, or cut into steaks, although smaller fish can be frozen whole. See page 14 for best methods of preparing for freezing.	3 months

FOOD	PACKAGING/PREPARATION	STORAGE TIME
Crab and lobster	Always cook before freezing. May be frozen whole in the shell, or the meat may be removed and stored. See page 14 for best methods of preparing for freezing.	1 month
Oysters and scallops	Usually frozen uncooked. Remove from the shells and reserve the juices. Wash thoroughly in salted water. Pack in rigid containers, with the reserved natural juices, leaving about 2.5 cm/1 inch headspace.	1 month
Prawns and shrimps (shrimp)	Can be either frozen already cooked, or washed in salted water and frozen uncooked. Pack in rigid containers, leaving about 1 cm/½ inch headspace, or in polythene (plastic) bags. Storage time is the same for cooked and uncooked.	1 month

MEAT

FOOD	PACKAGING/PREPARATION	STORAGE TIME
Beef Large joints (cuts)	May be frozen boned or on the bone. If storing on the bone, pad any portion of protruding bones with foil to prevent them piercing the outer wrapping. Wrap tightly in foil and seal. Many freezer owners give added protection to joints (cuts) on the bone by overwrapping them in stockinette.	8 months
Steaks	Braising or stewing steak can either be frozen whole (and treated as above), or cut into cubes and then stored in usable quantities. Always remove as much excess fat as possible before storing. Pack in polythene (plastic) bags. For steaks such as T-bone, sirloin, entrecôte, etc., interleave individual steaks with foil or film and overwrap tightly with foil.	6 months
Mince (ground meat)	Most bought mince (ground meat) is rather fatty and the best freezing results are achieved when you mince (grind) your own from braising or stewing steak, from which as much fat as possible has been removed. Pack in polythene (plastic) bags, in usable quantities.	2 months

FOOD	PACKAGING/PREPARATION	STORAGE TIME
Sausages	Most bought sausages contain seasoning and quite a lot of fat and are therefore suitable only for short-term freezing. Pack in polythene (plastic) bags, in usable quantities, or pack in rigid containers, interleaving the layers with foil or film.	1 month
Cooked beef	See under individual recipes. Stews and casseroles are usually packed in rigid containers. If there is any liquid, allow between 2.5 cm/1 inch and 1 cm/½ inch headspace. Storage time to some extent depends on individual ingredients. Dishes containing bacon, for example, have a shorter freezer life than those which do not.	About 2 months
Lamb Large joints (cuts)	*See* beef joints above. Remove any excess fat from legs or shoulders.	6 months
Chops, Stewing	*See* beef steaks above.	6 months
Cooked	*See* cooked beef above.	About 2 months
Pork Large joints (cuts)	Pork is a very fatty meat and therefore will keep for a shorter time than the leaner beef or lamb. Trim off as much excess fat as possible, otherwise see beef joints above.	4 months
Chops, Fillet (tender-loin)	*See* beef steak above.	3 months
Cooked	*See* cooked beef above.	6 weeks
Veal Large joints (cuts)	*See* beef joints above.	6 months
Chops, Stewing and Escalopes (scallops)	Trim off excess fat, otherwise see beef steaks above.	4 months
Cooked	*See* cooked beef above.	2 months

FOOD	PACKAGING/PREPARATION	STORAGE TIME
Bacon	Bacon does not freeze well and at best should be considered only for short-term storage. Wrap joints (cuts) tightly in foil, then overwrap in polythene (plastic) bags. Wrap rashers (slices) in foil, in usable quantities, and overwrap in polythene (plastic) bags. Vacuum-packed bacon can go straight in the freezer.	Smoked joints (cuts) and rashers (slices): 2 months Unsmoked joints (cuts): 5 weeks Unsmoked rashers (slices), chops and steaks: 2–3 weeks Vacuum-packed bacon: 4–5 months

FOOD	PACKAGING/PREPARATION	STORAGE TIME
Offal (variety meats)	Trim and, if necessary, wash thoroughly and pat dry. Remove any membranes. Wrap in cling film or foil, then pack in polythene (plastic) bags. Interleave individual liver slices with foil or film, then overwrap with foil, in usable quantities.	Liver: 2 months Other offal (variety meat): 3 months
Cooked	*See* cooked beef above.	2 months

POULTRY AND GAME

FOOD	PACKAGING/PREPARATION	STORAGE TIME
Whole poultry birds	Clean, remove heads, claws and any feathers. Tie legs together close to the body, then the wings. Pad any protruding bones with foil to prevent them from piercing the outer wrapping. Never stuff whole birds – stuffing keeps for a much shorter time than uncooked poultry and therefore shortens freezer life. Remove giblets before freezing unless you plan only short-term freezing (i.e. up to 2 months). Pack tightly in foil, then overwrap in polythene (plastic) bags and seal.	Chicken and turkey: 12 months Duck and goose: 6 months
Poultry, serving portions	Wrap individually in foil or cling film then pack in containers or polythene (plastic) bags.	*See* whole poultry birds above
Small whole game	Make sure game has been hung for the necessary time to produce the characteristic flavour before freezing. Preferably it should also be skinned and drawn. Pack as for poultry birds above.	6 months
Rabbit and hare, portions	Rabbit and hare can be frozen whole, but since they are usually cooked and eaten in portions, it is useful (and takes up less valuable freezer space) to freeze them already cut into serving portions. Bleed, then skin and drain. Wash each portion thoroughly and pat dry. Wrap each portion separately in foil or cling film, then pack in polythene (plastic) bags.	6 months
Venison, joints (cuts)	The meat should be hung for the appropriate time before freezing. Pack as for beef joints (cuts) above.	12 months

29

Steamed fruit puddings freeze very well and can be reheated from frozen in the steamer.

Thawing

How long frozen food takes to thaw depends on the type of food, the packaging, shape and size. The method of thawing can also vary. There are, however, some general guidelines which you may find helpful to follow.

1. The act of warming frozen food to room temperature again will restart the growth of the micro-organisms which promote deterioration. Food should therefore be consumed as quickly as possible after thawing – certainly within a day or two.

2. You will find suggestions, both in the charts which precede this section and in the recipes which follow, as to whether specific foods or dishes should be thawed in the refrigerator or at room temperature. To some extent this is a matter of individual preference and need, since it will depend on how quickly you wish to use the food. There is one general rule which should be considered before you decide just how you are going to defrost: thaw at room temperature only food which can completely defrost in less than 6 hours; anything which looks as if it might take much longer (large poultry birds or joints of meat, for instance), should, for safety's sake, be thawed in the refrigerator.

3. Some foods can be reheated straight from frozen – vegetables for instance, and certain foods (cooked or uncooked) which either have liquid stored with them or are, in fact, frozen liquid. Reheat straight from frozen over a very low heat, taking care to stir occasionally to prevent from sticking to the bottom of the pan. Casseroles and pies can be reheated in the oven in much the same way, but allow a little longer cooking time.

Here is a rough thawing guide for the major types of food:

Baked foods

Cakes and pastries are best thawed, in their wrapping, at room temperature for approximately 1 to 4 hours, depending on size. The one exception to this general rule is cakes with icing (frosting) or iced pastries – it is best to remove the wrapping before the thawing process begins, to avoid spoiling the appearance of the cake. Thaw cakes filled or decorated with cream in the refrigerator where possible.

Baked pies and flans can be put into the oven straight from frozen and reheated (see individual recipes for specific cooking times) unless they are to be eaten cold, in which case either thaw in the refrigerator or at room temperature. Allow about 2 hours for thawing at room temperature and approximately double that time for the refrigerator. Unbaked pies and flans can be put into the oven straight from frozen, but allow about 15 minutes on top of the normal cooking time.

Bread can be thawed either in the refrigerator or at room temperature. To crisp the crust, heat the bread in the oven for about 10 minutes after it has been completely thawed. Bread to be used for toasting can be toasted straight from frozen, allowing a little longer cooking time. Always thaw unbaked doughs in the refrigerator, otherwise they may over-rise, and leave overnight for the best results.

Dairy products
Most dairy products should be defrosted in the refrigerator, and only immediately before they are about to be used. As a rough average, about 0.5 kg/1 lb in weight will take 8 to 12 hours to thaw. The one exception to the general rule is eggs, which may be thawed, in their containers, either in the refrigerator or at room temperature. But they should be used within one day of thawing.

Fish
Most fish can be thawed either in the refrigerator or at room temperature. It will take about 6 to 8 hours for 0.5 kg/1 lb of fish to defrost in the refrigerator and about 3 to 5 hours at room temperature. Most fish are best thawed still in their wrapping. Smaller fish, fillets and steaks need not be thawed at all if they are to be cooked before eating – just cook straight from frozen in the usual way, allowing a little extra time for cooking. Any fish to be coated in breadcrumbs or any sort of batter must be thawed before being coated and cooked, since the coatings will not adhere to the frozen fish. All shellfish, with the exception of prawns or shrimps, should preferably be thawed in the refrigerator before being eaten or cooked. Allow about 6 to 8 hours thawing time. Shrimps or prawns can either be defrosted, or cooked straight from frozen in boiling liquid, but allow an extra minute or two on the cooking time.

Fruit
Fruit should always be thawed, unopened, in its container. For best results, thaw in the refrigerator. If you wish a faster thaw, it can be defrosted at room temperature or by placing the container in lukewarm water or under cold running water. This latter method will thaw the fruit in 30 to 45 minutes. General thawing times will depend not only on the type of fruit being thawed and the quantity, but also on the freezing method employed; dry-packed and syrup-packed fruit will take longer to thaw than sugar-packed. On average, however, allow 6 to 8 hours for 1 lb of fruit in the refrigerator, and about 2 to 4 hours at room temperature. Fruit being served uncooked for desserts should be served still slightly chilled for the best results. Fruit for stewing or pie fillings can be heated straight from frozen (see individual chart entries for specific details).

Meat
Small cuts of meat may be thawed either in the refrigerator or at room temperature; larger joints (cuts) and any cut of pork should be defrosted in the refrigerator. Always defrost meat in its wrapping, otherwise the juices will drip as the meat thaws, resulting in a loss of colour and flavour. Thawing in the refrigerator is a slow process, at least 5 hours per 1 lb of meat should be allowed for a complete thaw – although thawing at room temperature takes about half that time. Larger joints (cuts) of meat *can* be cooked straight from frozen, using the slow roasting method, but the cooked joint (cut) will be tougher than a similar joint (cut) cooked straight from fresh. Do not cook the meat at more than 180°C/350°F/Gas Mark 4 if you are cooking from frozen, and allow about 35 to 45 minutes per 0.5 kg/1 lb for beef and lamb, and about 50 minutes to 1 hour per 0.5 kg/1 lb for pork and veal. For best results when cooking from frozen, always use a meat thermometer to make sure the centre of the roast has been completely cooked; there is a danger that the outside parts of the meat will cook and brown quite quickly while the centre remains raw. Temperature readings on a meat thermometer should be 71°C/160°F for beef (medium), 82°C/180°F for lamb and 88°C/190°F for pork.

Smaller cuts of meat, such as steaks or chops can also be cooked from frozen allowing a longer cooking time, but again the resulting cooked meat will be tougher than if it had been cooked from fresh or defrosted. If minced (ground) meat is to be added to liquids or sauces in cooking, it can be added straight from frozen, providing you stir it occasionally to make sure it breaks up as it thaws out, and does not stick to the bottom of the pan. Meat with a particularly short life when fresh, such as minced (ground) meat and offal (variety meats) such as liver, should always be cooked and eaten immediately they are thawed. For specific thawing and cooking instructions for cooked meats, see the individual recipes which follow. As a general guideline, stews or casseroles which contain gravy or other liquid can be heated straight from frozen. Other cooked meats without sauces should be thawed in their containers in the refrigerator before using.

Poultry and game
If possible, all uncooked poultry and game should be defrosted in their wrapping in the refrigerator for, like pork, poultry and game are particularly susceptible to contamination as they warm up. Since it can take up to several days to thaw out a really large turkey this may not always be practicable, and the process can be speeded up either by immersing the bird, still in its wrappings, in cold (not hot) running water, or by defrosting it at room temperature – providing that it is cooked immediately on completion of the thawing process. Thawing time for whole poultry or game birds can take from about 1 day for a game bird or chicken weighing less than 2 kg/4½ lb, to 3 days for a 9 kg/20 lb turkey. Poultry portions and rabbit and hare portions should also be defrosted in their wrapping in the refrigerator. Allow 4 to 8 hours for thawing, depending on the size of the portions. Cooked poultry and game should be thawed in the same way as cooked meat.

Vegetables
Most vegetables do not need to be thawed at all before cooking. They can be plunged straight into boiling water from frozen. Since the blanching process partially cooks them, they will require shorter cooking times than if they were being cooked straight from fresh. For specific instructions for individual vegetables, see the vegetable freezing chart entries on page 16.

If you wish to steam vegetables from frozen, they should be partially thawed so that they can be separated. Steaming times are approximately the same as the boiling times given in the vegetable freezing chart. Stew and casserole vegetables can be added to their dishes frozen and cooked in the usual way.

Béchamel sauce

*Béchamel sauce

METRIC/IMPERIAL
600 ml/1 pint milk
1 onion, stuck with a few
  cloves
1 carrot, quartered
1 celery stick, chopped
1 bay leaf
6 peppercorns
25 g/1 oz butter
25 g/1 oz flour
salt
freshly ground black
  pepper

AMERICAN
2½ cups milk
1 onion, stuck with a few
  cloves
1 carrot, quartered
1 celery stalk, chopped
1 bay leaf
6 peppercorns
2 tablespoons butter
¼ cup flour
salt
freshly ground black
  pepper

Put the milk, vegetables, bay leaf and peppercorns into a saucepan and bring to the boil. Cover the pan, remove from the heat and set aside for 20 minutes. Strain the milk into a jug.

Melt the butter in a saucepan and stir in the flour to make a smooth paste. Cook for 1 minute. Stir in the strained milk and bring to the boil, stirring continuously. Simmer for 2 to 3 minutes, or until the sauce has thickened and is smooth. Stir in salt and pepper to taste.

To freeze: cool quickly and pour into rigid containers, in usable quantities. Cover, label and freeze.
Storage life: up to 6 months
To thaw and serve: turn into a saucepan and thaw over a very low heat. Bring to the boil, stirring continuously, and use according to recipe instructions.
Makes 600 ml/1 pint/2½ cups

*Chicken stock

METRIC/IMPERIAL	AMERICAN
2 chicken carcasses, broken into pieces	2 chicken carcasses, broken into pieces
2 sets of giblets, chopped	2 sets of giblets, chopped
1 large onion, sliced	1 large onion, sliced
1 leek, thoroughly cleaned and sliced	1 leek, thoroughly cleaned and sliced
2 carrots, sliced	2 carrots, sliced
1 × 5 ml spoon/ 1 teaspoon salt	1 teaspoon salt
10 peppercorns	10 peppercorns
1 bay leaf	1 bay leaf
2 parsley sprigs	2 parsley sprigs

Put the carcasses and giblets into a large saucepan and cover with cold water. Bring slowly to the boil, skimming the scum from the surface.

Add all the remaining ingredients, cover and simmer for 1½ hours, adding more water if necessary to keep the carcasses covered. Strain the stock.

To freeze: cool quickly, remove any fat from the surface and pour into rigid containers, in usable quantities. Cover, label and freeze. Or boil briskly until the stock has reduced by a third, then set aside to cool. Freeze in ice-cube trays. When frozen, put in polythene (plastic) bags, seal, label and return to the freezer.

Storage life: up to 6 months

To thaw and serve: add frozen to soups and casseroles, or turn into a saucepan and thaw over a very low heat.

*Mornay sauce

METRIC/IMPERIAL	AMERICAN
300 ml/½ pint béchamel sauce (see opposite page)	1¼ cups béchamel sauce (see opposite page)
50 g/2 oz Cheddar cheese, grated	½ cup grated Cheddar cheese
0.5 × 5 ml spoon made mustard (optional)	½ teaspoon made mustard (optional)
salt	salt
freshly ground black pepper	freshly ground black pepper

Pour the béchamel sauce into a saucepan and bring to the boil. Stir in the grated cheese, mustard if using, and salt and pepper to taste. Simmer until the cheese has melted, stirring continuously.

To freeze: cool quickly and pour into a rigid container. Cover, label and freeze.

Storage life: up to 3 months

To thaw and serve: turn into a saucepan and thaw over a very low heat. Cook until hot but not boiling, stirring continuously.

Makes 300 ml/½ pint/1¼ cups

*Apple sauce

METRIC/IMPERIAL	AMERICAN
0.5 kg/1 lb cooking apples, peeled, cored and sliced	1 lb baking apples, peeled, cored and sliced
4 × 15 ml spoons/ 4 tablespoons water	¼ cup water
25 g/1 oz butter	2 tablespoons butter

Put the apples, water and butter into a saucepan and bring to the boil. Cover and simmer for 15 minutes, stirring occasionally. Purée the mixture until smooth.

To freeze: cool quickly and turn into a rigid container. Cover, label and freeze.

Storage life: up to 6 months

To thaw and serve: melt 25 g/1 oz/2 tablespoons of butter in a saucepan and add the apple sauce. Thaw over a very low heat until hot, stirring continuously.

Makes about 0.5 kg/1 lb

*Beef stock

METRIC/IMPERIAL	AMERICAN
1.5 kg/3 lb beef bones	3 lb beef bones
3 carrots, sliced	3 carrots, sliced
2 onions, sliced	2 onions, sliced
1 leek, thoroughly cleaned and sliced	1 leek, thoroughly cleaned and sliced
2 bay leaves	2 bay leaves
2 parsley sprigs	2 parsley sprigs
1 × 5 ml spoon/ 1 teaspoon salt	1 teaspoon salt
10 peppercorns	10 peppercorns

Put the beef bones into a large saucepan and cover with cold water. Bring slowly to the boil, skimming the scum from the surface.

Add the vegetables and flavourings, cover and simmer for 3 hours, adding more water if necessary to keep the bones covered. Strain the stock.

To freeze: cool quickly, remove any fat from the surface and pour into rigid containers, in usable quantities. Cover, label and freeze. Or boil briskly until the stock has reduced by a third, then set aside to cool. Freeze in ice-cube trays. When frozen, put in polythene (plastic) bags, seal, label and return to the freezer.

Storage life: up to 6 months

To thaw and serve: add frozen to soups or casseroles, or turn into a saucepan and thaw over a very low heat.

Lemon curd

*Lemon curd

METRIC/IMPERIAL	AMERICAN
100 g/4 oz butter	½ cup butter
225 g/8 oz caster sugar	1 cup superfine sugar
finely grated rind and	finely grated rind and
juice of 2 large lemons	juice of 2 large lemons
2 large eggs	2 large eggs

Put the butter and sugar into a heatproof bowl and set over a pan of simmering water. Heat gently, stirring continuously until the mixture has melted.

Beat the lemon rind and juice and eggs together, then gradually beat into the butter mixture. Heat gently, stirring frequently for 30 minutes, or until the mixture thickens.

Pour into small rigid containers and set aside to cool.

To freeze: cover, label and freeze.

Storage life: up to 4 months

To thaw and serve: thaw for 2 to 3 hours at room temperature.

Makes about 300 ml/½ pint/1¼ cups

*Artichoke soup

METRIC/IMPERIAL	AMERICAN
0.5 kg/1 lb Jerusalem artichokes, peeled and chopped	1 lb Jerusalem artichokes, peeled and chopped
750 ml/1¼ pints chicken stock	3 cups chicken stock
1 small onion, chopped	1 small onion, chopped
2 celery sticks, chopped	2 celery stalks, chopped
1 bouquet garni	1 bouquet garni
1 bay leaf	1 bay leaf
25 g/1 oz butter	2 tablespoons butter
25 g/1 oz flour	¼ cup flour
300 ml/½ pint milk	1¼ cups milk
salt	salt
freshly ground black pepper	freshly ground black pepper
150 ml/¼ pint single cream	⅔ cup light cream

Put the artichokes, stock, onion, celery and herbs into a saucepan and bring to the boil. Simmer for about 45 minutes, or until the vegetables are tender. Remove the bouquet garni and bay leaf and strain and reserve the cooking liquid. Purée the vegetables in a blender.

Melt the butter in a second saucepan and stir in the flour to make a smooth paste. Cook for 1 minute. Stir in the reserved cooking liquid, milk, vegetable purée and salt and pepper to taste. Bring to the boil, stirring continuously. Simmer for 5 minutes, or until the soup is thick and smooth.

To freeze: cool quickly and turn into a rigid container. Cover, label and freeze.

Storage life: up to 3 months

To thaw and serve: turn the soup into a saucepan and thaw over a very low heat. Bring the mixture to the boil. Or thaw at room temperature, then heat and bring to the boil. Stir in the cream, simmer gently to heat through and adjust the seasoning before serving.

Serves 4

Clam chowder

This dish is a favourite American snack meal. If you prefer, mussels may be substituted for the clams, or you can make corn chowder by adding a 450 g/1 lb can of sweetcorn instead of the amount suggested below.

METRIC/IMPERIAL	AMERICAN
50 g/2 oz butter	¼ cup butter
1 onion, chopped	1 onion, chopped
3 potatoes, diced	3 potatoes, diced
450 ml/¾ pint milk	2 cups milk
1 × 400 g/14 oz can clams, drained	1 × 14 oz can clams, drained
1 × 175 g/6 oz can sweetcorn, drained	1 × 6 oz can corn kernels, drained
salt	salt
freshly ground black pepper	freshly ground black pepper
150 ml/¼ pint double cream	⅔ cup heavy cream
1 × 15 ml spoon/ 1 tablespoon butter	1 tablespoon butter

Melt the butter in a saucepan and add the onion and potatoes. Fry gently for 10 minutes. Stir in the milk, clams, corn and salt and pepper to taste and bring to the boil. Cover the pan and simmer for 10 to 15 minutes, or until the vegetables are tender.

To freeze: cool quickly and turn into a rigid container. Cover, label and freeze.

Storage life: up to 1 month

To thaw and serve: turn the chowder into a saucepan and thaw over a very low heat. Bring the mixture to the boil. Stir in the cream and butter and heat gently until the butter has melted and the soup is hot but not boiling.

Serves 6

Beef, bean and corn soup

*Beef, bean and corn soup

METRIC/IMPERIAL	AMERICAN
2 × 15 ml spoons/ 2 tablespoons olive oil	2 tablespoons olive oil
0.75 kg/1½ lb braising steak, cubed	1½ lb chuck steak, cubed
2 onions, chopped	2 onions, chopped
1 red pepper, deseeded and chopped	1 red pepper, deseeded and chopped
1 × 15 ml spoon/ 1 tablespoon paprika	1 tablespoon paprika
1.2 litres/2 pints beef stock	5 cups beef stock
1 × 400 g/14 oz can haricot beans, drained	1 × 14 oz can navy beans, drained
1 × 225 g/8 oz can sweetcorn, drained	1 × ½ lb can corn kernels, drained
225 g/8 oz garlic sausage, sliced	½ lb garlic sausage, sliced
salt	salt
freshly ground black pepper	freshly ground black pepper

Heat the oil in a saucepan and add the beef cubes. Fry until they are browned all over. Add the onions and red pepper and fry gently until they are soft. Stir in the paprika, then pour over the stock. Bring to the boil. Cover and simmer for 2 hours.

Add the remaining ingredients and stir to mix. Bring to the boil again. Cover and simmer for a further 30 minutes, or until the meat is cooked and very tender.

To freeze: cool quickly and turn into a rigid container. Cover, label and freeze.

Storage life: up to 2 months

To thaw and serve: turn into a saucepan and thaw over a very low heat. Bring the mixture to the boil, stirring occasionally.

Serves 6 to 8

Fish soup

METRIC/IMPERIAL	AMERICAN
50 g/2 oz butter	¼ cup butter
2 onions, chopped	2 onions, chopped
2 garlic cloves, crushed	2 garlic cloves, crushed
1 celery stick, chopped	1 celery stalk, chopped
2 × 15 ml spoons/	2 tablespoons tomato
2 tablespoons tomato	paste
purée	2 potatoes, chopped
2 potatoes, chopped	1 × 14 oz can tomatoes
1 × 400 g/14 oz can	2 teaspoons grated lemon
tomatoes	rind
2 × 5 ml spoons/	2½ cups chicken or
2 teaspoons grated lemon	fish stock
rind	2 bay leaves
600 ml/1 pint chicken or	salt
fish stock	freshly ground black
2 bay leaves	pepper
salt	6 oz haddock fillets,
freshly ground black	skinned and chopped
pepper	¼ lb cod fillets,
175 g/6 oz haddock fillets,	skinned and chopped
skinned and chopped	½ cup frozen shrimp,
100 g/4 oz cod fillets,	thawed
skinned and chopped	¼ cup grated Parmesan
100 g/4 oz frozen shrimps,	cheese to garnish
thawed	
25 g/1 oz grated Parmesan	
cheese to garnish	

Melt the butter in a saucepan and add the onion, garlic and celery. Fry gently until they are soft. Stir in the tomato purée (paste), potatoes, tomatoes, lemon rind, stock, bay leaves and salt and pepper to taste. Bring to the boil. Cover the pan and simmer for 15 minutes.

Stir in the chopped haddock and cod and simmer for 5 minutes. Stir in the shrimps, re-cover and simmer for 5 to 8 minutes or until the fish is cooked. Remove the bay leaves.

To freeze: cool quickly and turn into a rigid container. Cover, label and freeze.
Storage life: up to 1 month
To thaw and serve: turn the soup into a saucepan and thaw over a very low heat. Bring the mixture to the boil. Sprinkle over the Parmesan before serving.
Serves 6

*Avocado dip

METRIC/IMPERIAL	AMERICAN
2 avocado pears	2 avocado pears
juice of ½ lemon	juice of ½ lemon
1 × 15 ml spoon/	1 tablespoon olive oil
1 tablespoon olive oil	1 teaspoon mustard
1 × 5 ml spoon/	1 teaspoon superfine sugar
1 teaspoon mustard	salt
1 × 5 ml spoon/	freshly ground black
1 teaspoon caster sugar	pepper
salt	⅔ cup heavy cream
freshly ground black	
pepper	
150 ml/¼ pint double	
cream	

Cut the pears in half and remove the stones (seeds). Scoop out the flesh and transfer to a bowl. Mash well. Beat the remaining ingredients together until the cream forms stiff peaks. Fold into the avocado mixture.
To freeze: turn into a small rigid container. Cover, label and freeze.
Storage life: up to 2 months
To thaw and serve: thaw for 4 hours at room temperature. Serve with raw vegetable sticks, potato crisps (chips) and crackers.
Serves 6

Avocado dip

French potato soup

*French potato soup

This soup can be served hot, as here, for a filling winter soup, or it may be served slightly chilled as the summer soup, Vichyssoise.

METRIC/IMPERIAL	AMERICAN
0.5 kg/1 lb potatoes, cut into small pieces	*1 lb potatoes, cut into small pieces*
450 ml/¾ pint beef stock	*2 cups beef stock*
3 leeks, thoroughly cleaned and sliced	*3 leeks, thoroughly cleaned and sliced*
pinch of cayenne	*pinch of cayenne*
salt	*salt*
freshly ground black pepper	*freshly ground black pepper*
450 ml/¾ pint milk and cream, mixed	*2 cups milk and cream, mixed*
1 × 15 ml spoon/ 1 tablespoon chopped parsley to garnish	*1 tablespoon chopped parsley to garnish*

Put the potatoes and stock into a saucepan and bring to the boil. Cook for 10 minutes. Add the leek and cook for a further 10 minutes, or until the vegetables are tender. Purée the mixture in a blender, then stir in the cayenne and salt and pepper to taste.
To freeze: cool quickly and turn into a rigid container. Cover, label and freeze.
Storage life: up to 3 months
To thaw and serve: turn the soup into a saucepan and thaw over a very low heat. Stir in the milk and cream mixture and heat until hot but not boiling. Or thaw at room temperature, heat and stir in the milk and cream mixture. Garnish with chopped parsley before serving.
Serves 4

Gazpacho

*Gazpacho

Gazpacho

METRIC/IMPERIAL
*0.5 kg/1 lb tomatoes,
    blanched, peeled and
    chopped
2 shallots, grated
1 garlic clove, crushed
2 × 15 ml spoons/
    2 tablespoons lemon juice
1 × 15 ml spoon/
    1 tablespoon olive oil
450 ml/¾ pint tomato juice
salt
freshly ground black
    pepper*
To garnish:
*1 green pepper, deseeded
    and sliced
½ small cucumber, diced
croûtons*

AMERICAN
*1 lb tomatoes, blanched,
    peeled and chopped
2 shallots, grated
1 garlic clove, crushed
2 tablespoons lemon
    juice
1 tablespoon olive oil
2 cups tomato juice
salt
freshly ground black
    pepper*
To garnish:
*1 green pepper, deseeded
    and sliced
½ small cucumber, diced
croûtons*

Purée the tomatoes in a blender, then transfer to a large bowl. Stir in the shallots, garlic, lemon juice, oil, tomato juice and salt and pepper to taste. Beat well.
To freeze: turn into a rigid container, cover, label and freeze.
Storage life: up to 3 months
To thaw and serve: thaw overnight in the refrigerator, or for 5 hours at room temperature. Beat well and adjust the seasoning. Pour into a chilled serving bowl and serve with the garnishes.
Serves 4

French pork pâté

METRIC/IMPERIAL

50 g/2 oz butter or lard

0.5 kg/1 lb pig's liver, trimmed and coarsely minced

225 g/8 oz lean pork meat, coarsely minced

225 g/8 oz belly of pork, coarsely minced

2 garlic cloves, crushed

1 small onion, chopped

25 g/1 oz flour

150 ml/¼ pint beef stock

2 × 5 ml spoons/ 2 teaspoons chopped mixed herbs

pinch of grated nutmeg

salt

freshly ground black pepper

3 sage leaves

0.5 kg/1 lb streaky bacon, sliced

AMERICAN

¼ cup butter or lard

1 lb pork liver, trimmed and coarsely ground

½ lb lean pork meat, coarsely ground

½ lb belly of pork, coarsely ground

2 garlic cloves, crushed

1 small onion, chopped

¼ cup flour

⅔ cup beef stock

2 teaspoons chopped mixed herbs

pinch of grated nutmeg

salt

freshly ground black pepper

3 sage leaves

1 lb fatty bacon, sliced

Melt the butter or lard in a large frying pan and add the meat, garlic and onion. Fry gently until the meat loses its pinkness. Stir in the flour to make a smooth paste and cook for 1 minute. Stir in the stock, herbs, nutmeg and salt and pepper to taste. Bring to the boil, stirring continuously. Simmer for 3 minutes, or until the mixture is thick and smooth.

Arrange the sage leaves on the bottom of an oven-proof dish or terrine. Line the bottom and sides with the bacon slices and spoon in the pâté. Cover tightly with foil. Stand in a roasting pan and pour in enough boiling water to come half-way up the sides. Bake in a preheated moderate oven (160°C/325°F, Gas Mark 3) for 1¼ hours, or until the pâté shrinks from the edge of the dish. Set aside to cool quickly, with a weight on top of the dish.

To freeze: remove the weight and turn out of the dish or terrine. Wrap in heavy-duty foil. Put in a polythene (plastic) bag, seal, label and freeze.

Storage life: up to 6 weeks

To thaw and serve: thaw overnight in the refrigerator. Serve with hot toast and butter.

Serves 8 to 10

French pork pâté

*Smoked mackerel pâté

METRIC/IMPERIAL	AMERICAN
2 large smoked mackerel, skinned and boned	2 large smoked mackerel, skinned and boned
5 × 15 ml spoons/ 5 tablespoons rich cream cheese	⅓ cup rich cream cheese
juice of ½ lemon	juice of ½ lemon
275 g/10 oz butter, melted	1¼ cups butter, melted
salt	salt
freshly ground black pepper	freshly ground black pepper
parsley sprigs to garnish	parsley sprigs to garnish

Purée the mackerel in a blender or mash thoroughly with a fork. Transfer to a large bowl and stir in the remaining ingredients until the mixture is smooth and well blended.

To freeze: turn into a rigid container, cover, label and freeze. Or freeze in a rigid container, turn out and wrap in heavy-duty foil, then put in a polythene (plastic) bag, seal, label and freeze.

Storage life: up to 2 months

To thaw and serve: thaw overnight in the refrigerator or for 4 hours at room temperature. Garnish with the parsley and serve with hot toast and butter.

Serves 6

Kidney cream soup

METRIC/IMPERIAL	AMERICAN
50 g/2 oz butter	¼ cup butter
1 onion, chopped	1 onion, chopped
4 lambs' kidneys, trimmed and chopped	4 lamb kidneys, trimmed and chopped
300 ml/½ pint beef stock	1¼ cups beef stock
25 g/1 oz cornflour	¼ cup cornstarch
150 ml/¼ pint milk	⅔ cup milk
1 × 2.5 ml spoon/ ½ teaspoon grated nutmeg	½ teaspoon grated nutmeg
salt	salt
freshly ground black pepper	freshly ground black pepper
3 × 15 ml spoons/ 3 tablespoons sherry	3 tablespoons sherry
150 ml/¼ pint double cream	⅔ cup heavy cream

Melt the butter in a saucepan and add the onion and kidneys. Fry gently until they are evenly browned. Stir in the stock and bring to the boil. Cover the pan and simmer for 20 minutes.

Blend the cornflour (cornstarch) and milk together to make a smooth paste. Stir into the kidney mixture and add the nutmeg and salt and pepper to taste. Cook for 5 minutes, stirring continuously. Stir in the sherry.

To freeze: cool quickly and turn into a rigid container. Cover, label and freeze.

Storage life: up to 2 months

To thaw and serve: turn the soup into a saucepan and thaw over a very low heat. Stir in the cream and heat until hot but not boiling.

Serves 4

Quick pâté

METRIC/IMPERIAL	AMERICAN
5 rashers streaky bacon	5 slices fatty bacon
100 g/4 oz fresh breadcrumbs	2 cups fresh breadcrumbs
1 egg	1 egg
4 × 15 ml spoons/ 4 tablespoons dry sherry	¼ cup dry sherry
225 g/8 oz chicken livers, chopped	½ lb chicken livers, chopped
1 garlic clove, peeled	1 garlic clove, peeled
225 g/8 oz pig's liver, trimmed and chopped	½ lb pork liver, trimmed and chopped
salt	salt
freshly ground black pepper	freshly ground black pepper
pinch of grated nutmeg	pinch of grated nutmeg
1 × 5 ml spoon/1 teaspoon dried mixed herbs	1 teaspoon dried mixed herbs
100 g/4 oz bacon trimmings, in small pieces (or use 100 g/ 4 oz bacon, chopped)	¼ lb bacon trimmings, in small pieces (or use ¼ lb bacon chopped)
100 g/4 oz butter, melted	½ cup butter, melted

Line the bottom and sides of a medium loaf tin (pan) or terrine with the bacon rashers (slices). Put the breadcrumbs, egg, sherry and chicken livers in a blender and purée. Transfer to a bowl.

Purée the remaining ingredients, except the butter, in the blender, then transfer to the bowl. Stir in the melted butter and blend well.

Spoon the pâté into the loaf tin (pan) or terrine and cover tightly with foil. Stand in a roasting pan and pour in enough boiling water to come half-way up the sides. Bake in a preheated moderate oven (160°C/ 325°F, Gas Mark 3) for 2 hours, or until the pâté shrinks from the edge of the dish. Set aside to cool.

To freeze: turn out of the tin (pan) or terrine. Wrap in heavy-duty foil. Put in a polythene (plastic) bag, seal, label and freeze.

Storage life: up to 2 months

To thaw and serve: thaw for 6 hours at room temperature. Serve with hot toast and butter.

Serves 4

Kipper pâté : Liver pâté

*Kipper pâté

METRIC/IMPERIAL	AMERICAN
350 g/12 oz boil-in-bag kipper fillets	¾ lb boil-in-bag kipper fillets
2 × 5 ml spoons/ 2 teaspoons lemon juice	2 teaspoons lemon juice
1 × 15 ml spoon/ 1 tablespoon horseradish sauce	1 tablespoon horseradish sauce
salt	salt
freshly ground black pepper	freshly ground black pepper
225 g/8 oz butter, softened	1 cup butter, softened

Cook the kippers according to packet instructions. Drain and reserve about 4 × 15 ml spoons/4 tablespoons/¼ cup of the juices. Skin, bone and flake the fish. Put the fish and juices, lemon juice, horseradish and salt and pepper to taste into a blender and blend to a purée.

Transfer the mixture to a bowl and beat in the butter until it is thoroughly blended. Adjust the seasoning.

To freeze: turn into a rigid container, cover, label and freeze.

Storage life: up to 2 months

To thaw and serve: thaw overnight in the refrigerator or for 5 hours at room temperature. Spoon into a serving bowl and serve with hot toast or crusty bread.
Serves 6

Liver pâté

METRIC/IMPERIAL	AMERICAN
225 g/8 oz pig's liver, trimmed and minced	½ lb pork liver, trimmed and ground
225 g/8 oz belly of pork, minced	½ lb belly of pork, ground
1 garlic clove, crushed	1 garlic clove, crushed
salt	salt
freshly ground black pepper	freshly ground black pepper
1 × 5 ml spoon/ 1 teaspoon dried thyme	1 teaspoon dried thyme
2 × 15 ml spoons/ 2 tablespoons red wine	2 tablespoons red wine
4 rashers streaky bacon	4 slices fatty bacon

Mix the liver and pork together. Stir in the garlic, salt and pepper to taste, thyme and wine. Turn into a small ovenproof dish or terrine. Cover the pâté with the bacon rashers (slices), then cover tightly with foil. Stand in a roasting pan and pour in enough boiling water to come half-way up the sides. Bake in a preheated moderate oven (160°C/325°F, Gas Mark 3) for 1¼ hours, or until the pâté shrinks from the edge of the dish. Pour off excess fat. Set aside to cool.

To freeze: turn out of the dish or terrine and wrap in heavy-duty foil. Put in a polythene (plastic) bag, seal, label and freeze.

Storage life: up to 2 months

To thaw and serve: thaw overnight in the refrigerator. Serve with toast or crusty bread.
Serves 6

Onion soup

Onion soup

METRIC/IMPERIAL	AMERICAN
50 g/2 oz butter	¼ cup butter
0.5 kg/1 lb onions, finely chopped	1 lb onions, finely chopped
25 g/1 oz flour	¼ cup flour
900 ml/1½ pints beef stock	3¾ cups beef stock
2 × 5 ml spoons/ 2 teaspoons tomato purée	2 teaspoons tomato paste
salt	salt
freshly ground black pepper	freshly ground black pepper
6 slices French bread, lightly toasted	6 slices French bread, lightly toasted
3 garlic cloves, halved	3 garlic cloves, halved
50 g/2 oz Cheddar or Gruyère cheese, grated	½ cup grated Cheddar or Gruyère cheese

Melt the butter in a saucepan, add the chopped onion and fry gently until soft. Stir in the flour to make a smooth paste and cook for 1 minute. Stir in the stock, tomato purée (paste) and salt and pepper to taste. Bring back to the boil, stirring continuously. Cover the pan and simmer for 40 minutes.
To freeze: cool quickly and turn into a rigid container. Cover, label and freeze.
Storage life: up to 4 months
To thaw and serve: turn the soup into a saucepan and thaw over a very low heat. Bring the mixture to the boil. Or thaw at room temperature, heat and bring to the boil. Rub both sides of the bread with the garlic clove halves and float the slices on top of the soup. Sprinkle the cheese generously over the bread. Cook in a preheated hot oven (220°C/425°F, Gas Mark 7) until the cheese has melted. Ladle into individual bowls and float the bread slices on top.
Serves 6

Watercress soup

METRIC/IMPERIAL	AMERICAN
50 g/2 oz butter	¼ cup butter
2 onions, finely chopped	2 onions, finely chopped
1 large potato, chopped	1 large potato, chopped
225 g/8 oz watercress, chopped	½ lb watercress, chopped
600 ml/1 pint chicken stock	2½ cups chicken stock
salt	salt
freshly ground black pepper	freshly ground black pepper
450 ml/¾ pint creamy milk	2 cups creamy milk
watercress sprigs to garnish	watercress sprigs to garnish

Melt the butter in a saucepan. Add the onions and potato, cover and cook gently for 5 minutes. Add half the watercress and cook for another 3 minutes. Stir in the stock and salt and pepper to taste. Cover and simmer for 20 to 25 minutes or until the vegetables are tender. Remove from the heat and push through a sieve (strainer). Add the remaining watercress.
To freeze: cool quickly and turn into a rigid container. Cover, label and freeze.
Storage life: up to 3 months
To thaw and serve: turn the soup into a saucepan with the milk and thaw over a very low heat. To serve chilled, thaw overnight in the refrigerator, or for 4 to 5 hours at room temperature, then stir in the milk. Adjust the seasoning and garnish individual bowls with a watercress sprig.
Serves 4 to 6

*Ratatouille

METRIC/IMPERIAL	AMERICAN
4 × 15 ml spoons/ 4 tablespoons olive oil	¼ cup olive oil
2 medium onions, sliced	2 medium onions, sliced
1 garlic clove, crushed	1 garlic clove, crushed
2 green peppers, deseeded and sliced	2 green peppers, deseeded and sliced
1 large aubergine, sliced	1 large eggplant, sliced
4 courgettes, sliced	4 zucchini, sliced
1 × 0.75 kg/1½ lb can tomatoes	1 × 1½ lb can tomatoes
1 × 5 ml spoon/ 1 teaspoon dried basil	1 teaspoon dried basil
1 × 15 ml spoon/ 1 tablespoon chopped parsley	1 tablespoon chopped parsley
salt	salt
freshly ground black pepper	freshly ground black pepper

Heat the oil in a saucepan and add the onions and garlic. Fry gently until they are soft. Stir in the green peppers and aubergine (eggplant) and fry for 3 minutes. Stir in the courgettes (zucchini), tomatoes, herbs and salt and pepper to taste. Bring to the boil. Cover the pan and simmer for 45 minutes, or until the vegetables are tender.
To freeze: cool quickly and turn into a rigid container. Cover, label and freeze.
Storage life: up to 3 months
To thaw and serve: turn into a baking dish and put into a preheated moderate oven (180°C/350°F, Gas Mark 4). Cook for 30 minutes. Or thaw overnight in the refrigerator and serve cold.
Serves 6

Salmon mousse

METRIC/IMPERIAL	AMERICAN
1 × 0.5 kg/1 lb can salmon	1 × 1 lb can salmon
2 × 15 ml spoons/ 2 tablespoons lemon juice	2 tablespoons lemon juice
2 × 5 ml spoons/ 2 teaspoons tomato ketchup	2 teaspoons tomato catsup
1 × 15 ml spoon/ 1 tablespoon chopped parsley	1 tablespoon chopped parsley
salt	salt
freshly ground black pepper	freshly ground black pepper
4 × 15 ml spoons/ 4 tablespoons hot water	¼ cup hot water
1 × 15 ml spoon/ 1 tablespoon powdered gelatine	1 tablespoon powdered gelatin
1 × 175 g/6 oz can evaporated milk, chilled	1 × 6 oz can evaporated milk, chilled
2 egg whites, stiffly beaten	2 egg whites, stiffly beaten

Mash the salmon to a smooth paste, then stir in the lemon juice, ketchup (catsup), parsley and salt and pepper to taste.

Put the water into a heatproof bowl and sprinkle over the gelatine. Set the bowl over a pan of simmering water and stir until the gelatine has dissolved. Remove from the heat and beat into the salmon mixture.

Beat the evaporated milk until it has almost doubled in volume, then fold into the salmon mixture with the egg whites. Turn the mixture into a lightly oiled 1.2 litre/2 pint/5 cup freezerproof ring mould.

To freeze: open freeze. When frozen, wrap in heavy-duty foil. Put in a polythene (plastic) bag, seal, label and return to freezer.

Storage life: up to 6 months

To thaw and serve: turn the mould onto a serving dish and thaw for 3 to 4 hours at room temperature. Fill the centre with shredded lettuce and surround with cucumber slices before serving.

Serves 8

Scallops au gratin

METRIC/IMPERIAL	AMERICAN
8 scallops, cleaned and deveined	8 scallops, cleaned and deveined
120 ml/4 fl oz dry white wine	½ cup dry white wine
25 g/1 oz butter	2 tablespoons butter
25 g/1 oz flour	¼ cup flour
300 ml/½ pint milk	1¼ cups milk
75 g/3 oz Cheddar cheese, grated	¾ cup grated Cheddar cheese
1 egg yolk	1 egg yolk
2 × 15 ml spoons/ 2 tablespoons double cream	2 tablespoons heavy cream
salt	salt
freshly ground black pepper	freshly ground black pepper
1 kg/2 lb potatoes, cooked and mashed	2 lb potatoes, cooked and mashed

Put the scallops and wine into a saucepan and bring to the boil. Simmer gently for 10 minutes. Remove the scallops from the pan and boil the wine rapidly until it has reduced to about 1 × 15 ml spoon/1 tablespoon.

Melt the butter in a saucepan and stir in the flour to make a smooth paste. Cook for 1 minute. Stir in the milk and bring to the boil, stirring continuously. Stir in the reserved wine and 50 g/2 oz/½ cup of the grated cheese until the cheese melts. Blend the egg yolk and cream together and add to the sauce with the salt and pepper to taste. Heat through gently until it is hot but not boiling. Set aside.

Pipe the mashed potatoes in a border round 4 deep scallop shells. Divide the sauce between the shells. Cut the scallops into quarters and arrange them in the sauce. Sprinkle over the remaining cheese.

To freeze: cool quickly, then open freeze. When frozen, pack each shell into a polythene (plastic) bag, seal, label and return to freezer.

Storage life: up to 1 month

To thaw and serve: cook gently under a medium grill (broiler) for 20 minutes. Turn up to high, for final 5 minutes, to brown.

Serves 4

Salmon mousse ; Savoury crêpes

Savoury crêpes

METRIC/IMPERIAL
Batter:
100 g/4 oz plain flour
pinch of salt
1 egg
300 ml/½ pint milk
1 × 15 ml spoon/
  1 tablespoon melted
  butter
1 × 15 ml spoon/
  1 tablespoon cooking oil
Filling:
25 g/1 oz butter
50 g/2 oz mushrooms,
  sliced
300 ml/½ pint béchamel
  sauce (see page 32)
1 × 15 ml spoon/
  1 tablespoon chopped
  chives
175 g/6 oz peeled shrimps
1 × 15 ml spoon/
  1 tablespoon dry sherry
2 × 15 ml spoons/
  2 tablespoons double
  cream
salt
freshly ground black
  pepper

AMERICAN
Batter:
1 cup all-purpose flour
pinch of salt
1 egg
1¼ cups milk
1 tablespoon melted
  butter
1 tablespoon cooking oil

Filling:
2 tablespoons butter
½ cup sliced mushrooms
1¼ cups béchamel sauce
  (see page 32)
1 tablespoon chopped
  chives
¾ cup shelled shrimp
1 tablespoon dry sherry
2 tablespoons heavy cream
salt
freshly ground black
  pepper

To make the batter, sift the flour and salt into a bowl. Make a well in the centre and add the egg, then gradually beat in the milk. Stir in the melted butter and beat well. Set aside for 30 minutes.

Lightly brush the bottom of a medium frying pan (skillet) with a little oil. Set over a moderate heat and pour in enough batter just to cover the base of the pan thinly. Cook until the underside is golden brown, turn and cook the other side until golden brown. Repeat, using the remaining oil to grease the pan between each crêpe. Stack the crêpes on top of each other.

Melt the butter in a frying pan (skillet) and add the mushrooms. Fry gently until soft. Heat the béchamel sauce in a saucepan, then stir in the mushrooms and remaining filling ingredients. Heat until hot but not boiling. Spread the crêpes with the filling and roll up or fold.

To freeze: cool quickly and pack in foil containers, separating the layers with heavy-duty foil. Cover, label and freeze.

Storage life: up to 6 weeks

To thaw and serve: put frozen crêpes on a baking sheet, brush with melted butter and put into a pre-heated moderate oven (180°C/350°F, Gas Mark 4). Bake for 35 minutes.

Serves 6

Melon cocktail

Mustard dip

METRIC/IMPERIAL
225 g/8 oz rich cream
 cheese
4 × 15 ml spoons/
 4 tablespoons chopped
 mango chutney
pinch of dry mustard
1 × 5 ml spoon/
 1 teaspoon curry powder

AMERICAN
1 cup rich cream cheese
4 tablespoons chopped
 mango chutney
pinch of dry mustard
1 teaspoon curry powder

Mix all the ingredients together until they are thoroughly blended.
To freeze: turn into a rigid container, cover, label and freeze.
Storage life: up to 3 months
To thaw and serve: thaw for 8 hours in the refrigerator. Serve with potato crisps (chips) or frankfurters.
Serves 6

*Vegetable soup

METRIC/IMPERIAL
1 knuckle of bacon
25 g/1 oz dripping or lard
1 large onion, chopped
3 carrots, chopped
2 potatoes, chopped
3 celery sticks, sliced
2 bay leaves
salt
freshly ground black
 pepper
100 g/4 oz frozen peas

AMERICAN
1 knuckle of smoked ham
2 tablespoons drippings or
 lard
1 large onion, chopped
3 carrots, chopped
2 potatoes, chopped
3 celery stalks, sliced
2 bay leaves
salt
freshly ground black
 pepper
¼ lb frozen peas

Soak the bacon (ham) overnight and drain. Put into a saucepan and just cover with water. Bring to the boil, then drain off the water. Pour over 1.2 litres/2 pints/ 5 cups of fresh cold water and bring to the boil. Simmer for 40 minutes.

Melt the dripping or lard in a saucepan and add the onion, carrots, potatoes and celery. Fry gently until the vegetables are soft. Drain the cooking liquid from the bacon (ham) and add to the pan and simmer for 30 minutes. Remove the skin and fat from the bacon (ham) and cut the meat into small pieces. Add to the soup with the peas and simmer for a further 5 minutes.
To freeze: cool quickly, turn into a rigid container, cover, label and freeze.
Storage life: up to 4 months
To thaw and serve: turn the soup into a saucepan and thaw over a very low heat. Bring the mixture to the boil, stirring occasionally. Or thaw overnight in the refrigerator, heat and bring to the boil.
Serves 6

Melon cocktail

METRIC/IMPERIAL
1 small ripe melon,
 skinned and deseeded
2 × 15 ml spoons/
 2 tablespoons lime juice
150 ml/¼ pint sweet white
 wine

AMERICAN
1 small ripe melon,
 skinned and deseeded
2 tablespoons lime juice
⅔ cup sweet white wine

To garnish:
4 mint sprigs
lemon slices

To garnish:
4 mint sprigs
lemon slices

Using a vegetable scoop, make balls of the melon flesh and put them into a rigid container. Pour over the lime juice and wine.
To freeze: cover, label and freeze.
Storage life: up to 4 months
To thaw and serve: thaw overnight in the refrigerator. Spoon into individual serving glasses and garnish each one with a mint sprig and lemon slice.
Serves 4

*Taramasalata

METRIC/IMPERIAL	AMERICAN
225 g/8 oz smoked cod's roe, skinned	½ lb smoked cod's roe, skinned
2 small slices white bread, crusts removed	2 small slices white bread, crusts removed
2 × 15 ml spoons/ 2 tablespoons milk	2 tablespoons milk
5 × 15 ml spoons/ 5 tablespoons olive oil	⅓ cup olive oil
2 × 15 ml spoons/ 2 tablespoons lemon juice	2 tablespoons lemon juice
salt	salt
freshly ground black pepper	freshly ground black pepper
1 garlic clove, crushed (optional)	1 garlic clove, crushed (optional)
chopped parsley to garnish	chopped parsley to garnish

Put the roe in a mortar or bowl and pound with a pestle or mash with a fork until smooth. Soak the bread in the milk, then squeeze out as much milk as possible. Add to the cod's roe and mash again. Beat in the oil, 1 × 5 ml spoon/1 teaspoon at a time, then gradually beat in the lemon juice, salt and pepper to taste and garlic, if liked.

To freeze: spoon into a rigid container, cover, label and freeze.

Storage life: up to 1 month

To thaw and serve: thaw overnight in the refrigerator or for 3 hours at room temperature. Serve with toast, or with black olives and pitta (Greek bread), sprinkled with chopped parsley.

Serves 4

Smoked salmon flan

METRIC/IMPERIAL	AMERICAN
175 g/6 oz frozen shortcrust pastry, thawed	6 oz frozen basic pie dough, thawed
Filling:	**Filling:**
2 eggs	2 eggs
150 ml/¼ pint single cream	⅔ cup light cream
4 × 15 ml spoons/ 4 tablespoons milk	¼ cup milk
pinch of grated nutmeg	pinch of grated nutmeg
salt	salt
freshly ground black pepper	freshly ground black pepper
100 g/4 oz smoked salmon, cut into strips	¼ lb smoked salmon, cut into strips

Roll out the pastry dough on a lightly floured surface and use to line a well-greased 20 cm/8 inch flan dish (pie pan). Put the dish (pan) on a baking sheet.

Beat the eggs, cream and milk together and add the nutmeg and salt and pepper to taste. Arrange the salmon strips over the bottom of the pastry case (pie shell) and pour over the cream mixture.

Put the sheet into a preheated moderately hot oven (190°C/375°F, Gas Mark 5) and bake for 35 to 40 minutes, or until the filling is set and the pastry golden brown.

To freeze: cool quickly, turn out of the flan dish (pie pan) and pack in a polythene (plastic) bag. Seal, label and place carefully in the freezer.

Storage life: up to 1 month

To thaw and serve: turn the flan into the dish (pan) and put into a preheated moderate oven (180°C/350°F, Gas Mark 4) for 30 minutes.

Serves 6

Taramasalata

FISH

Fish pie

METRIC/IMPERIAL
0.5 kg/1 lb cod or haddock
 fillets, skinned and
 halved
300 ml/½ pint milk
300 ml/½ pint water
50 g/2 oz butter
25 g/1 oz flour
3 hard-boiled eggs,
 chopped
1 × 2.5 ml spoon/
 ½ teaspoon grated
 nutmeg
salt
freshly ground black
 pepper
0.75 kg/1½ lb potatoes,
 cooked and mashed
1 egg, beaten
75 g/3 oz Cheddar cheese,
 grated
milk
parsley sprigs to garnish

AMERICAN
1 lb cod or haddock
 fillets, skinned and
 halved
1¼ cups milk
1¼ cups water
¼ cup butter
¼ cup flour
3 hard-cooked eggs,
 chopped
½ teaspoon grated
 nutmeg
salt
freshly ground black
 pepper
1½ lb potatoes, cooked and
 mashed
1 egg, beaten
¾ cup grated Cheddar
 cheese
milk
parsley sprigs to garnish

Put the fish, milk and water into a saucepan and bring to the boil. Cover and simmer for 15 minutes, or until the fish is cooked. Remove the fish to a board. Strain and reserve 450 ml/¾ pint/2 cups of the liquid. Skin, bone and flake the fish. Set aside.

Melt half the butter in a saucepan and stir in the flour to make a smooth paste. Cook for 1 minute. Stir in the reserved cooking liquid and bring to the boil, stirring continuously. Simmer for 2 to 3 minutes. Stir in the fish, eggs, nutmeg and salt and pepper to taste. Spoon into a rigid container.

Blend together the mashed potatoes, beaten egg, remaining butter, two-thirds of the grated cheese and enough milk to make a smooth consistency. Spoon the mixture over the fish to cover it completely. Sprinkle over the remaining grated cheese.

To freeze: cool quickly, then open freeze. When frozen, cover, label and return to the freezer.
Storage life: up to 1 month
To thaw and serve: thaw overnight in the refrigerator or for 4 hours at room temperature. Remove the cover and put into a preheated hot oven (220°C/425°F, Gas Mark 7) for 30 minutes, or until the potatoes are lightly browned. Serve garnished with parsley sprigs.
Serves 4 to 6

*Kedgeree

METRIC/IMPERIAL
200 g/7 oz long-grain rice
salt
100 g/4 oz butter
1 large onion, chopped
350 g/12 oz smoked cod,
 cooked, skinned, boned
 and flaked
4 hard-boiled eggs,
 chopped
1 × 15 ml spoon/
 1 tablespoon chopped
 parsley
freshly ground black
 pepper
4 × 15 ml spoons/
 4 tablespoons single cream

AMERICAN
1 cup long-grain rice
salt
½ cup butter
1 large onion, chopped
¾ lb smoked cod, cooked,
 skinned, boned and
 flaked
4 hard-cooked eggs,
 chopped
1 tablespoon chopped
 parsley
freshly ground black
 pepper
¼ cup light cream

Cook the rice in boiling, salted water for 15 to 20 minutes, or until it is cooked and the liquid absorbed.

Melt the butter in a large saucepan and add the onion. Fry gently until soft. Stir in the fish, eggs, parsley, rice and salt and pepper to taste. Mix well.
To freeze: cool quickly and turn into a well-greased rigid foil container. Cover, label and freeze.
Storage life: up to 1 month
To thaw and serve: put into a preheated moderately hot oven (200°C/400°F, Gas Mark 6) for 50 minutes, stirring the rice occasionally. Stir in the cream before serving.
Serves 4

Kedgeree

Haddock in white wine sauce

METRIC/IMPERIAL	AMERICAN
25 g/1 oz butter	2 tablespoons butter
1 onion, chopped	1 onion, chopped
1 garlic clove, crushed	1 garlic clove, crushed
1 × 225 g/8 oz can tomatoes	1 × ½ lb can tomatoes
75 g/3 oz mushrooms, sliced	¾ cup sliced mushrooms
3 anchovies, chopped	3 anchovies, chopped
150 ml/¼ pint dry white wine	⅔ cup dry white wine
1 × 15 ml spoon/ 1 tablespoon chopped parsley	1 tablespoon chopped parsley
salt	salt
freshly ground black pepper	freshly ground black pepper
1 × 0.5 kg/1 lb packet frozen haddock fillets	1 × 1 lb package frozen haddock fillets
oil for shallow frying	oil for shallow frying

Melt the butter in a saucepan and add the onion and garlic. Fry gently until they are soft. Stir in the tomatoes, mushrooms, anchovies, wine, parsley and salt and pepper to taste, and bring to the boil. Simmer for 20 minutes, stirring occasionally.
To freeze: cool quickly and turn into a rigid container. Cover, label and freeze.
Storage life: up to 4 months
To thaw and serve: turn into a saucepan and thaw over a very low heat. Bring the mixture to the boil. Fry the haddock according to packet instructions, then transfer to a serving dish. Pour over the sauce.
Serves 4

*Seafood stew

METRIC/IMPERIAL	AMERICAN
0.5 kg/1 lb halibut	1 lb halibut
150 ml/¼ pint dry white wine	⅔ cup dry white wine
1 small onion, chopped	1 small onion, chopped
1 × 400 g/14 oz can condensed lobster bisque	1 × 14 oz can condensed lobster bisque
1 × 150 g/5 oz packet frozen dressed crab	1 × 5 oz package frozen dressed crab
100 g/4 oz frozen peeled shrimps, thawed	½ cup frozen shelled shrimp, thawed
1 × 15 ml spoon/ 1 tablespoon chopped parsley	1 tablespoon chopped parsley
salt	salt
freshly ground black pepper	freshly ground black pepper
0.75 kg/1½ lb potatoes, cooked and mashed	1½ lb potatoes, cooked and mashed
25 g/1 oz butter	2 tablespoons butter
milk	milk
lemon wedges to garnish	lemon wedges to garnish

Cod florentine

METRIC/IMPERIAL	AMERICAN
8 small cod fillets, skinned	8 small cod fillets, skinned
juice of ½ lemon	juice of ½ lemon
4 × 15 ml spoons/ 4 tablespoons dry white wine	¼ cup dry white wine
salt	salt
freshly ground black pepper	freshly ground black pepper
225 g/8 oz packet frozen spinach	½ lb package frozen spinach
25 g/1 oz butter	2 tablespoons butter
300 ml/½ pint béchamel sauce (see page 32)	1¼ cups béchamel sauce (see page 32)
2 × 15 ml spoons/ 2 tablespoons grated Parmesan cheese	2 tablespoons grated Parmesan cheese

Fold the fillets in half and arrange them in a well-greased ovenproof dish. Pour over the lemon juice, wine and salt and pepper to taste. Cover and put into a preheated moderately hot oven (190°C/375°F, Gas Mark 5). Cook for 15 to 20 minutes, or until the fish is cooked. Transfer the fish to a plate and reserve the cooking liquid.

Cook the spinach according to packet instructions, then stir in the butter. Arrange the mixture on the bottom of a rigid foil container and put the fish on top. Heat the béchamel sauce, then stir in about 2 × 15 ml spoons/2 tablespoons of the reserved cooking liquid. Pour over the fish, then sprinkle over the grated cheese.
To freeze: cool quickly, cover, label and freeze.
Storage life: up to 1 month
To thaw and serve: thaw uncovered for 3 hours at room temperature. Put into a preheated moderately hot oven (200°C/400°F, Gas Mark 6) for 40 minutes or until the top is golden brown.
Serves 4

Put the halibut, wine and onion into a saucepan and bring to the boil. Cover and simmer for 10 minutes. Transfer the fish to a board. Skin and bone the fish. Stir the bisque into the cooking liquid and simmer for 2 minutes. Stir in the fish, crab, shrimps, parsley and salt and pepper to taste. Bring to the boil, stirring continuously. Set aside.

Beat the potatoes, butter and enough milk together to make a smooth consistency. Pipe the potatoes round the edge of a well-greased rigid foil container. Spoon the fish mixture into the centre.
To freeze: cool quickly, then open freeze. When frozen, cover, label and return to the freezer.
Storage life: up to 1 month
To thaw and serve: thaw for 4 hours at room temperature or overnight in the refrigerator. Put, uncovered, into a preheated hot oven (220°C/425°F, Gas Mark 7) for 30 to 40 minutes, or until the potatoes are golden. Garnish with the lemon wedges.
Serves 6

Fish cakes

METRIC/IMPERIAL
0.75 kg/1½ lb smoked fish
  fillets
300 ml/½ pint water
150 ml/¼ pint milk
0.75 kg/1½ lb potatoes,
  cooked and mashed
2 × 15 ml spoons/
  2 tablespoons chopped
  parsley
freshly ground black
  pepper
1 × 5 ml spoon/1 teaspoon
  mustard
15 g/½ oz butter
15 g/½ oz flour
1 egg, beaten
100 g/4 oz dry
  breadcrumbs
oil for deep frying

AMERICAN
1½ lb smoked fish fillets
1¼ cups water
⅔ cup milk
1½ lb potatoes, cooked and
  mashed
2 tablespoons chopped
  parsley
freshly ground black
  pepper
1 teaspoon mustard
1 tablespoon butter
2 tablespoons flour
1 egg, beaten
1 cup dry breadcrumbs
oil for deep frying

Put the fish, water and milk into a saucepan and bring to the boil. Cover the pan and simmer for 15 minutes or until the fish is cooked. Remove the fish to a board. Strain and reserve 150 ml/¼ pint/⅔ cup of the cooking liquid. Skin, bone and flake the fish, then transfer it to a bowl. Beat in the potatoes, parsley, pepper and mustard.

Melt the butter in a small saucepan and stir in the flour to make a smooth paste. Cook for 1 minute. Stir in the reserved cooking liquid and bring to the boil, stirring continuously. Simmer for 2 to 3 minutes. Bind the fish mixture with as much sauce as necessary then divide into 12 portions. Shape into flat, round cakes. Brush with beaten egg, then coat thoroughly in breadcrumbs.

To freeze: put into a polythene (plastic) bag or rigid container, separating the layers with heavy-duty foil. Cover or seal, label and freeze.

Storage life: up to 1 month

To thaw and serve: thaw for 1 hour in the refrigerator, then deep fry in hot oil until golden brown. Drain on paper towels and serve hot.

Serves 6

Fish cakes

Plaice (flounder) in cider

Plaice (flounder) in cider

METRIC/IMPERIAL
8 plaice fillets, skinned
1 small onion, chopped
25 g/1 oz butter
25 g/1 oz flour
300 ml/½ pint cider
1 × 15 ml spoon/
 1 tablespoon mustard
1 × 15 ml spoon/
 1 tablespoon chopped
 parsley
1 × 2.5 ml spoon/
 ½ teaspoon brown sugar
salt
freshly ground black
 pepper
parsley sprigs to garnish

AMERICAN
8 flounder fillets, skinned
1 small onion, chopped
2 tablespoons butter
¼ cup flour
1¼ cups hard cider or
 unsweetened apple juice
1 tablespoon mustard
1 tablespoon chopped
 parsley
½ teaspoon brown sugar
salt
freshly ground black
 pepper
parsley sprigs to garnish

Fold the fillets in half and arrange them in a well-greased ovenproof dish. Sprinkle over the onion.

Melt the butter in a saucepan and stir in the flour to make a smooth paste. Cook for 1 minute. Stir in the cider and bring to the boil, stirring continuously. Simmer for 2 to 3 minutes. Stir in the mustard, parsley, sugar and salt and pepper to taste. Pour the sauce over the fish. Put the dish into a preheated moderately hot oven (190°C/375°F, Gas Mark 5). Cook for 10 to 15 minutes or until the fish is cooked.

To freeze: cool quickly and carefully transfer the mixture to a rigid foil container. Cover, label and freeze.

Storage life: up to 1 month

To thaw and serve: thaw, covered, for 3 hours at room temperature, then put into a preheated moderately hot oven (190°C/375°F, Gas Mark 5) for 1 hour. Serve garnished with parsley sprigs.

Serves 4

Paella

METRIC/IMPERIAL
120 ml/4 fl oz olive oil
2 onions, chopped
2 garlic cloves, crushed
2 celery sticks, sliced
400 g/14 oz long-grain rice
1 × 2.5 ml spoon/
  ½ teaspoon ground
  saffron
1 × 0.75 kg/1½ lb can
  tomatoes, drained
900 ml/1½ pints chicken
  stock
2.25 kg/5 lb chicken, cut
  into serving portions
100 g/4 oz streaky bacon,
  chopped
225 g/8 oz peeled shrimps
150 g/5 oz frozen peas,
  thawed
100 g/4 oz cooked mussels,
  shelled
salt
freshly ground black
  pepper

AMERICAN
½ cup olive oil
2 onions, chopped
2 garlic cloves, crushed
2 celery stalks, sliced
2 cups long-grain rice
½ teaspoon ground saffron
1 × 1½ lb can tomatoes,
  drained
3¾ cups chicken stock
5 lb chicken, cut into
  serving portions
¼ lb fatty bacon,
  chopped
1 cup shelled shrimp
5 oz frozen peas, thawed
¼ lb cooked mussels,
  shelled
salt
freshly ground black
  pepper

Heat half the oil in a saucepan and add the onions, garlic and celery. Fry gently until they are soft. Stir in the rice and saffron and cook for 3 minutes, stirring continuously. Stir in the tomatoes and stock, and bring to the boil. Simmer for 10 minutes, stirring occasionally.

Heat the remaining oil in a saucepan and add the chicken pieces. Fry until they are browned all over. Add the bacon and fry until crisp. Stir the chicken and bacon into the rice with the remaining ingredients. Simmer for 10 to 15 minutes, or until the rice is cooked and the liquid is absorbed. (It should still be slightly moist for best freezing results.)

To freeze: cool quickly and pack into polythene (plastic) bags. Seal, label and freeze.

Storage life: up to 1 month

To thaw and serve: thaw for 4 hours at room temperature, then turn into a well-greased ovenproof dish. Cover and put into a preheated moderately hot oven (190°C/375°F, Gas Mark 5) for 45 minutes, stirring occasionally.
Serves 8 to 10

Salmon quiches

METRIC/IMPERIAL
375 g/13 oz frozen
  shortcrust pastry,
  thawed
Filling:
1 × 225 g/8 oz can red
  salmon, bones removed
  drained and flaked
100 g/4 oz cooked peeled
  prawns, chopped
100 g/4 oz cream cheese,
  softened
3 eggs, beaten
150 ml/¼ pint milk
juice of ½ lemon
pinch of cayenne
salt
chopped parsley to garnish

AMERICAN
13 oz frozen basic pie
  dough, thawed
Filling:
1 × ½ lb can red salmon,
  bones removed,
  drained and flaked
¼ lb cooked shelled
  shrimp, chopped
¼ lb cream cheese,
  softened
3 eggs, beaten
⅔ cup milk
juice of ½ lemon
pinch of cayenne
salt
chopped parsley to garnish

Lightly grease six 13 cm/5 inch shallow (or 7.5 cm/3 inch deep) fluted flan tins (tart pans) with removable bases. Roll out the pastry on a lightly floured surface and use to line the flan tins (tart pans). Chill for at least 15 minutes in the refrigerator.

To make the filling, put the salmon and prawns (shrimp) in a mixing bowl and add the remaining ingredients, except the chopped parsley. Mix together well and pour the filling into the prepared pastry cases (tart shells).

To freeze: Place on baking sheets and open freeze. When frozen, remove from the freezer and leave for a few minutes at room temperature. Carefully ease the quiches out of the tins (pans). Wrap in heavy-duty foil, then overwrap in a polythene (plastic) bag. Seal, label and return to the freezer.

Storage life: up to 1 month

To thaw and serve: unwrap and replace in the flan tins (tart pans). Place on baking sheets, cover with foil and put in a preheated, moderately hot oven (190°C/375°F, Gas Mark 5) for 45 minutes. Remove the foil and continue baking for 15 minutes or until golden brown. Serve sprinkled with chopped parsley.
Makes 6 individual quiches

Sole bonne femme

METRIC/IMPERIAL
8 sole fillets, skinned
150 ml/¼ pint fish stock
150 ml/¼ pint dry white
  wine
40 g/1½ oz butter
50 g/2 oz mushrooms,
  sliced
25 g/1 oz flour
5 × 15 ml spoons/
  5 tablespoons double
  cream
salt
freshly ground black
  pepper

AMERICAN
8 sole fillets, skinned
⅔ cup fish stock
⅔ cup dry white wine
3 tablespoons butter
½ cup sliced mushrooms
¼ cup flour
⅓ cup heavy cream
salt
freshly ground black
  pepper

Fold the fillets in half and arrange in a well-greased ovenproof dish. Pour over the stock and wine. Cover and put into a preheated moderate oven (160°C/325°F, Gas Mark 3). Poach for 20 to 25 minutes, or until the fish is cooked. Transfer the fillets to a rigid foil container. Drain the cooking liquid and reserve 250 ml/8 fl oz/1 cup.

To make the sauce, melt 15 g/½ oz/1 tablespoon of butter in a frying pan (skillet) and add the mushrooms. Fry gently until they are soft. Remove from the heat. Melt the remaining butter in a saucepan and stir in the flour to make a smooth paste. Cook for 1 minute. Stir in the reserved cooking liquid and bring to the boil, stirring continuously. Stir in most of the mushrooms, the cream and salt and pepper to taste and simmer for 2 to 3 minutes. Spoon over the fillets and top with the remaining mushrooms.

To freeze: cool quickly, cover, label and freeze.
Storage life: up to 1 month
To thaw and serve: put the container, covered, into a preheated cool oven (150°C/300°F, Gas Mark 2) for 30 minutes.
Serves 4

*Shrimps provençale

METRIC/IMPERIAL
25 g/1 oz butter
1 small onion, chopped
1 garlic clove, crushed
0.5 kg/1 lb tomatoes,
  blanched, peeled and
  deseeded
2 × 5 ml spoons/
  2 teaspoons chopped
  parsley
1 × 15 ml spoon/
  1 tablespoon sherry
1 × 5 ml spoon/
  1 teaspoon chopped
  chives
225 g/8 oz peeled shrimps
salt
freshly ground black
  pepper
chopped parsley to garnish

AMERICAN
2 tablespoons butter
1 small onion, chopped
1 garlic clove, crushed
1 lb tomatoes, blanched,
  peeled and deseeded
2 teaspoons chopped
  parsley
1 tablespoon sherry
1 teaspoon chopped
  chives
1 cup shelled shrimp
salt
freshly ground black
  pepper
chopped parsley to garnish

Melt the butter in a saucepan and add the onion and garlic. Fry gently until they are soft. Stir in the tomatoes and simmer until they are soft but still retain their shape. Stir in the parsley, sherry, chives, shrimps and salt and pepper to taste. Bring to the boil. Simmer for 5 minutes.

To freeze: cool quickly and turn into a polythene (plastic) boil-in-bag. Seal, label and freeze. Or turn into a small rigid container, cover, label and freeze.
Storage life: up to 1 month
To thaw and serve: put the bag into a saucepan of boiling water and simmer gently until thawed, then boil for 10 minutes. Or turn the mixture into a saucepan and thaw gently over a very low heat. Bring to the boil. Serve over rice and garnished with chopped parsley.
Serves 2

Whiting Véronique

METRIC/IMPERIAL
4 large whiting fillets,
  skinned and halved
juice of ½ lemon
150 ml/¼ pint dry white
  wine
1 small onion, chopped
2 parsley sprigs
salt
freshly ground black
  pepper
25 g/1 oz butter
25 g/1 oz flour
175 g/6 oz white grapes,
  halved and deseeded
300 ml/½ pint single cream

AMERICAN
4 large whiting fillets,
  skinned and halved
juice of ½ lemon
⅔ cup dry white wine
1 small onion, chopped
2 parsley sprigs
salt
freshly ground black
  pepper
2 tablespoons butter
¼ cup flour
6 oz white grapes,
  halved and deseeded
1¼ cups light cream

Fold the fillets in half and arrange in a well-greased ovenproof dish. Pour over the lemon juice and wine and add the onion, parsley and salt and pepper to taste. Add just enough water to cover the fish. Cover and put into a preheated moderately hot oven (190°C/375°F, Gas Mark 5). Cook for 20 minutes, or until the fish is cooked. Transfer the fish to a rigid foil container. Boil the cooking liquid until it reduces to 4 × 15 ml spoons/4 tablespoons/¼ cup.

To make the sauce, melt the butter in a saucepan and stir in the flour to make a smooth paste. Cook for 1 minute. Stir in the reserved cooking liquid and bring to the boil, stirring continuously. Simmer for 2 to 3 minutes. Stir in the grapes and cream and salt and pepper to taste. Reheat but do not boil. Spoon over the fillets.

To freeze: cool quickly, cover, label and freeze.
Storage life: up to 1 month
To thaw and serve: thaw, uncovered, for 4 hours at room temperature. Cover and put into a preheated moderate oven (180°C/350°F, Gas Mark 4) for 40 to 50 minutes.
Serves 4

Shrimps provençale

MEAT

Barbecued lamb chops

METRIC/IMPERIAL	AMERICAN
50 g/2 oz butter	¼ cup butter
2 small onions, chopped	2 small onions, chopped
2 garlic cloves, crushed	2 garlic cloves, crushed
1 × 400 g/14 oz can tomatoes	1 × 14 oz can tomatoes
2 × 15 ml spoons/ 2 tablespoons tomato purée	2 tablespoons tomato paste
1 × 15 ml spoon/ 1 tablespoon brown sugar	1 tablespoon brown sugar
2 × 15 ml spoons/ 2 tablespoons wine vinegar	2 tablespoons wine vinegar
salt	salt
freshly ground black pepper	freshly ground black pepper
4 large lamb chops	4 large lamb chops

Melt the butter in a saucepan and add the onions and garlic. Fry gently until they are soft. Stir in all the remaining ingredients, except the chops, and bring to the boil. Cover and simmer for 15 minutes, stirring occasionally.

Rub the chops all over with salt and pepper, then arrange them in a rigid foil container. Spoon the sauce over the meat. Put the dish into a preheated moderate oven (180°C/350°F, Gas Mark 4) and bake for 45 minutes.

To freeze: cool quickly, cover, label and freeze.
Storage life: up to 2 months
To thaw and serve: put, uncovered, into a preheated moderate oven (180°C/350°F, Gas Mark 4) for 45 minutes.
Serves 4

*Beef carbonnades

METRIC/IMPERIAL	AMERICAN
1 kg/2 lb braising steak, cubed	2 lb chuck steak, cubed
50 g/2 oz seasoned flour	½ cup seasoned flour
50 g/2 oz butter	¼ cup butter
3 onions, sliced	3 onions, sliced
1 garlic clove, crushed	1 garlic clove, crushed
15 g/½ oz flour	2 tablespoons flour
300 ml/½ pint ale or stout	1¼ cups beer or stout
150 ml/¼ pint beef stock	⅔ cup beef stock
1 × 2.5 ml spoon/ ½ teaspoon sugar	½ teaspoon sugar
1 × 5 ml spoon/ 1 teaspoon malt vinegar	1 teaspoon malt vinegar
2 bay leaves	2 bay leaves
1 × 5 ml spoon/ 1 teaspoon dried thyme	1 teaspoon dried thyme
salt	salt
freshly ground black pepper	freshly ground black pepper

Beef kromeskies

METRIC/IMPERIAL	AMERICAN
50 g/2 oz butter	¼ cup butter
50 g/2 oz flour	½ cup flour
300 ml/½ pint beef stock	1¼ cups beef stock
225 g/8 oz cooked roast beef, chopped	½ lb cooked roast beef, chopped
1 egg, beaten	1 egg, beaten
1 × 15 ml spoon/ 1 tablespoon chopped parsley	1 tablespoon chopped parsley
salt	salt
freshly ground black pepper	freshly ground black pepper
oil for deep frying	oil for deep frying
Coating:	**Coating:**
25 g/1 oz seasoned flour	¼ cup seasoned flour
1 egg, beaten	1 egg, beaten
50 g/2 oz dry breadcrumbs	½ cup dry breadcrumbs

Melt the butter and stir in the flour to make a smooth paste. Cook for 1 minute. Stir in the stock and bring to the boil, stirring continuously. Simmer for 2 minutes. Remove from the heat and stir in the beef, egg, parsley and salt and pepper to taste. Set aside to cool completely.

Divide the mixture into 8 equal portions. Coat in the flour, then in the beaten egg and finally in the breadcrumbs.

To freeze: turn into a rigid container, cover, label and freeze.
Storage life: up to 2 months
To thaw and serve: thaw overnight in the refrigerator. Deep fry the kromeskies in hot oil for 4 minutes, or until they are crisp and golden brown. Drain on paper towels and serve hot.
Serves 4

Coat the beef cubes in the flour. Melt the butter in a saucepan and add the beef cubes. Fry until they are browned all over. Transfer to a plate. Add the onions and garlic to the pan and fry gently until they are soft. Stir in the flour to make a smooth paste. Cook for 1 minute. Stir in the ale (beer) or stout and stock and bring to the boil, stirring occasionally. Stir in the remaining ingredients. Cover and simmer for 2 hours, or until the meat is cooked. Remove the bay leaves.

To freeze: cool quickly and turn into a rigid foil container. Cover, label and freeze.
Storage life: up to 2 months
To thaw and serve: put, covered, into a preheated moderately hot oven (200°C/400°F, Gas Mark 6) for 40 minutes.
Serves 6

Bacon, tomato and onion flan

Bacon, tomato and onion flan

METRIC/IMPERIAL	AMERICAN
175 g/6 oz frozen shortcrust pastry, thawed	*6 oz frozen basic pie dough, thawed*
25 g/1 oz butter	*2 tablespoons butter*
1 onion, chopped	*1 onion, chopped*
100 g/4 oz bacon, chopped	*¼ lb bacon, chopped*
1 egg	*1 egg*
salt	*salt*
freshly ground black pepper	*freshly ground black pepper*
150 ml/¼ pint single cream	*⅔ cup light cream*
2 tomatoes, sliced	*2 tomatoes, sliced*

Roll out the pastry dough on a lightly floured surface and use to line a well-greased 20 cm/8 inch flan dish (pie pan). Put the dish (pan) on a baking sheet.

Melt the butter in a frying pan (skillet) and add the onion. Fry gently until soft. Add the bacon and fry until golden brown. Beat the egg, salt and pepper and cream together. Arrange the bacon and onion in the pastry case (pie shell) and pour over the cream mixture. Arrange the tomato slices in a circle around the edge of the filling. Put the sheet into a preheated moderately hot oven (190°C/375°F, Gas Mark 5) and bake for 35 to 40 minutes, or until the filling is set and the pastry golden brown.

To freeze: cool quickly and turn out of the flan dish (pie pan) and pack in a polythene (plastic) bag. Seal, label and place carefully in the freezer.

Storage life: up to 6 weeks

To thaw and serve: turn the flan into the dish (pan) and put into a preheated moderate oven (180°C/350°F, Gas Mark 4) for 30 minutes.

Serves 4

Beef with dumplings

METRIC/IMPERIAL

2 × 15 ml spoons/
  2 tablespoons cooking oil
2 rashers streaky bacon,
  finely chopped
1 kg/2 lb braising steak,
  cubed
2 medium onions, chopped
3 medium carrots, chopped
150 ml/¼ pint stout
450 ml/¾ pint beef stock
salt
freshly ground black
  pepper
Dumplings:
100 g/4 oz self-raising
  flour
salt
freshly ground black
  pepper
65 g/2½ oz shredded beef
  suet
4 × 15 ml spoons/
  4 tablespoons water

AMERICAN

2 tablespoons cooking oil
2 slices fatty bacon,
  finely chopped
2 lb chuck steak, cubed
2 medium onions, chopped
3 medium carrots, chopped
⅔ cup stout or beer
2 cups beef stock
salt
freshly ground black
  pepper
Dumplings:
1 cup self-rising flour
salt
freshly ground black
  pepper
½ cup shredded beef
  suet
¼ cup water

Heat the oil in a frying pan (skillet) and add the bacon. Fry gently until it is crisp. Transfer it to a saucepan. Add the beef cubes to the frying pan (skillet) and fry until they are browned all over. Transfer the beef to the bacon and arrange the vegetables over the top. Add the stout or beer, stock, and salt and pepper to taste. Bring to the boil. Cover and simmer for 1½ hours.

Meanwhile, to make the dumplings, sift the flour and salt and pepper into a mixing bowl. Stir in the suet and enough water to make a smooth, soft dough. Roll the mixture into about 8 small balls and add them to the pan. Re-cover and simmer for a further 30 minutes, or until the beef is cooked.

To freeze: cool quickly and turn into a rigid foil container. Cover, label and freeze.

Storage life: up to 2 months

To thaw and serve: put, covered, into a preheated moderate oven (180°C/350°F, Gas Mark 4) for 1 hour.

Serves 4 to 6

*Beef goulash

METRIC/IMPERIAL

4 × 15 ml spoons/
  4 tablespoons cooking oil
1 large onion, chopped
2 garlic cloves, crushed
1 kg/2 lb braising steak,
  cubed
1 × 15 ml spoon/
  1 tablespoon paprika
1 × 400 g/14 oz can
  tomatoes
150 ml/¼ pint red wine or
  beef stock
1 × 5 ml spoon/
  1 teaspoon dried mixed
  herbs
6 small onions, peeled
6 small potatoes, scrubbed
6 small carrots, scraped
salt
freshly ground black
  pepper
150 ml/¼ pint sour cream
chopped parsley to
  garnish

AMERICAN

¼ cup cooking oil
1 large onion, chopped
2 garlic cloves, crushed
2 lb chuck steak, cubed
1 tablespoon paprika
1 × 14 oz can tomatoes
⅔ cup red wine or beef
  stock
½ teaspoon dried thyme
½ teaspoon dried oregano
6 small onions, peeled
6 small potatoes, scrubbed
6 small carrots, scraped
salt
freshly ground black
  pepper
⅔ cup sour cream
chopped parsley to
  garnish

Heat the oil in a saucepan and add the onion and garlic. Fry gently until they are soft. Add the beef cubes and fry until they are browned all over. Stir in the paprika until the meat is coated. Stir in the tomatoes, wine or stock and herbs and bring to the boil. Cover and simmer for 1½ hours. Stir in the onions, potatoes, carrots and salt and pepper to taste. Re-cover and simmer for a further 45 minutes, or until the beef is cooked.

To freeze: cool quickly and turn into a rigid container or polythene (plastic) bag. Cover or seal, label and freeze.

Storage life: up to 2 months

To thaw and serve: turn into a casserole, cover and put into a preheated moderate oven (160°C/325°F, Gas Mark 3) for 40 minutes. Stir in the sour cream and sprinkle with chopped parsley before serving.

Serves 4 to 6

Beef goulash

*Beef stroganoff

METRIC/IMPERIAL	AMERICAN
100 g/4 oz butter	*½ cup butter*
0.75 g/1½ lb fillet steak, cut into thin strips	*1½ lb boneless sirloin steak, cut into thin strips*
2 small onions, chopped	*2 small onions, chopped*
1 garlic clove, crushed	*1 garlic clove, crushed*
225 g/8 oz mushrooms, sliced	*2 cups sliced mushrooms*
5 × 15 ml spoons/ 5 tablespoons dry white wine	*⅓ cup dry white wine*
salt	*salt*
freshly ground black pepper	*freshly ground black pepper*
300 ml/½ pint sour cream	*1¼ cups sour cream*

Melt half the butter in a large frying pan (skillet) and add the steak strips. Fry briskly until they are browned all over. Transfer the strips to a rigid container. Add the remaining butter to the pan and add the onions and garlic. Fry gently until they are soft. Stir in the mushrooms, wine and salt and pepper to taste. Simmer for 5 minutes, or until the mushrooms are tender. Spoon over the meat.

To freeze: cool quickly, cover, label and freeze.
Storage life: up to 2 months
To thaw and serve: thaw for 4 hours at room temperature, then turn into a saucepan and heat gently, stirring occasionally, for 25 minutes. Stir in the sour cream before serving.
Serves 4

Beef bourguignonne

METRIC/IMPERIAL	AMERICAN
50 g/2 oz dripping or lard	*¼ cup drippings or lard*
1 kg/2 lb chuck steak, cubed	*2 lb chuck or round steak, cubed*
175 g/6 oz streaky bacon, rind removed and chopped	*6 oz fatty bacon, rind removed and chopped*
12 small onions or shallots, peeled	*12 baby onions or shallots, peeled*
1 garlic clove, crushed	*1 garlic clove, crushed*
2 × 15 ml spoons/ 2 tablespoons flour	*2 tablespoons flour*
300 ml/½ pint Burgundy wine	*1¼ cups Burgundy wine*
150 ml/¼ pint beef stock	*⅔ cup beef stock*
2 carrots, sliced	*2 carrots, sliced*
1 bouquet garni	*1 bouquet garni*
salt	*salt*
freshly ground black pepper	*freshly ground black pepper*
225 g/8 oz button mushrooms	*2 cups button mushrooms*

Melt the dripping or lard in a saucepan, add the steak cubes and fry until they are browned all over. Drain and place in a casserole. Add the bacon to the pan and fry briskly, then stir in the onions or shallots and garlic and fry for 1 minute. Sprinkle in the flour and cook, stirring occasionally. Gradually stir in the wine and stock and bring to the boil, stirring. Transfer to the casserole and add the carrots, bouquet garni and salt and pepper to taste. Put, covered, into a preheated moderate oven (160°C/325°F, Gas Mark 3) for 1½ hours, adding extra stock if necessary. Add the mushrooms and cook for another 30 minutes.

To freeze: cool quickly and turn into a rigid container. Cover, label and freeze.
Storage life: up to 2 months
To thaw and serve: turn into a casserole, cover and put into a preheated moderate oven (180°C/350°F, Gas Mark 4) for 1 to 1½ hours.
Serves 4 to 6

Chicken in cider

METRIC/IMPERIAL	AMERICAN
0.5 kg/1 lb boiling bacon, soaked overnight and drained	*1 lb unprocessed smoked ham, scrubbed*
1 bay leaf	*1 bay leaf*
1 onion, quartered	*1 onion, quartered*
1.5 kg/3 lb chicken, with giblets	*3 lb chicken, with giblets*
1 onion, sliced	*1 onion, sliced*
3 carrots, sliced	*3 carrots, sliced*
4 celery sticks, sliced	*4 celery stalks, sliced*
salt	*salt*
freshly ground black pepper	*freshly ground black pepper*
300 ml/½ pint dry cider	*1¼ cups hard cider*
600 ml/1 pint water	*2½ cups water*
40 g/1½ oz butter	*3 tablespoons butter*
40 g/1½ oz flour	*⅓ cup flour*

Put the bacon (ham) into a saucepan and cover with fresh water. Add the bay leaf and onion. Bring to the boil, cover and simmer for 40 minutes. Put the chicken and giblets in a second pan and add the vegetables, salt and pepper, cider and water. Bring to the boil, cover and simmer for 40 minutes. Transfer the chicken and bacon to a working surface. Reserve the vegetables and stock from the chicken. Cut the bacon and chicken into small cubes, discarding skin, bones and gristle.

Melt the butter in a saucepan and stir in the flour to make a smooth paste. Cook for 1 minute. Strain the reserved stock, then stir into the paste. Bring to the boil, stirring continuously. Simmer for 2 minutes, then stir in the meats and vegetables.

To freeze: cool quickly and turn into a rigid container. Cover, label and freeze.
Storage life: up to 6 weeks
To thaw and serve: turn into a heavy casserole and put into a preheated moderate oven (160°C/325°F, Gas Mark 3) for 40 minutes, stirring occasionally.
Serves 6 to 8

Beef ragoût with prunes

*Beef ragoût with prunes

METRIC/IMPERIAL
600 ml/1 pint beef stock
225 g/8 oz prunes
0.75 kg/1½ lb braising
  steak, cubed
25 g/1 oz seasoned flour
4 × 15 ml spoons/
  4 tablespoons cooking oil
1 × 400 g/14 oz can
  tomatoes
2 × 15 ml spoons/
  2 tablespoons tomato
  purée
1 bouquet garni
1 bay leaf
salt
freshly ground black
  pepper

AMERICAN
2½ cups beef stock
½ lb prunes
1½ lb chuck steak, cubed
¼ cup seasoned flour
¼ cup cooking oil
1 × 14 oz can tomatoes
2 tablespoons tomato
  paste
1 bouquet garni
1 bay leaf
salt
freshly ground black
  pepper

Pour the stock into a saucepan and bring to the boil. Pour over the prunes and set aside to soak for 12 hours (if you are using tenderized prunes, soak for only 1 hour).

Coat the beef cubes in the seasoned flour. Heat the oil in a saucepan and add the meat cubes. Fry until they are browned all over. Strain the stock from the prunes and pour into the pan. Bring to the boil. Stir in the tomatoes, tomato purée (paste), herbs, salt and pepper to taste and about half the prunes. Cover and simmer for 1¾ hours. Stir in the remaining prunes, re-cover the pan and simmer for a further 15 minutes, or until the beef is cooked.

To freeze: cool quickly and turn into a rigid foil container. Cover, label and freeze.

Storage life: up to 2 months

To thaw and serve: put into a preheated moderate oven (180°C/350°F, Gas Mark 4) for 30 minutes. Serves 4

Cannelloni

Cannelloni

METRIC/IMPERIAL
8 cannelloni tubes
1 × 15 ml spoon/
  1 tablespoon olive oil
Filling:
2 × 15 ml spoons/
  2 tablespoons olive oil
1 large onion, chopped
2 garlic cloves, crushed
225 g/8 oz minced beef
100 g/4 oz minced chicken
  livers
1 × 225 g/8 oz can
  tomatoes
2 × 15 ml spoons/
  2 tablespoons tomato
  purée
4 × 15 ml spoons/
  4 tablespoons red wine
2 × 5 ml spoons/
  2 teaspoons dried basil
salt
freshly ground black
  pepper
Sauce:
25 g/1 oz butter
25 g/1 oz flour
300 ml/½ pint milk
50 g/2 oz grated Parmesan
  or Cheddar cheese
1 × 2.5 ml spoon/
  ½ teaspoon dry mustard
salt
freshly ground black
  pepper

AMERICAN
8 cannelloni tubes
1 tablespoon olive oil

Filling:
2 tablespoons olive oil
1 large onion, chopped
2 garlic cloves, crushed
½ lb ground beef
¼ lb ground chicken livers
1 × ½ lb can tomatoes
2 tablespoons tomato
  paste
¼ cup red wine
2 teaspoons dried basil
salt
freshly ground black
  pepper

Sauce:
2 tablespoons butter
¼ cup flour
1¼ cups milk
½ cup grated Parmesan
  or Cheddar cheese
½ teaspoon dry mustard
salt
freshly ground black
  pepper

First make the filling. Heat the oil in a saucepan and add the onion and garlic. Fry gently until they are soft. Add the beef and chicken livers and fry until they lose their pinkness. Stir in all the remaining filling ingredients and bring to the boil, stirring continuously. Cover and simmer for 30 minutes. Meanwhile, cook the cannelloni tubes in boiling water, to which the oil has been added, until they are just tender. Drain. Remove the filling from the heat and divide it between the tubes. Carefully arrange the stuffed tubes in a shallow ovenproof dish.

To make the sauce, melt the butter in a saucepan and stir in the flour to make a smooth paste. Cook for 1 minute. Stir in the milk and bring to the boil, stirring continuously. Simmer for 2 to 3 minutes. Stir in the grated cheese, mustard and salt and pepper to taste. When the cheese has melted, pour the sauce over the stuffed tubes.

To freeze: cool quickly, then open freeze. When frozen, turn out of the dish and put into a polythene (plastic) bag. Seal, label and return to the freezer.
Storage life: up to 2 months
To thaw and serve: put the mixture in an ovenproof dish and place in a preheated moderately hot oven (200°C/400°F, Gas Mark 6) for 1 hour, or until the sauce is lightly browned.
Serves 4

Blanquette de veau

METRIC/IMPERIAL	AMERICAN
1 kg/2 lb lean stewing veal, cubed	*2 lb lean stewing veal, cubed*
2 onions, quartered	*2 onions, quartered*
2 carrots, quartered	*2 carrots, quartered*
2 bay leaves	*2 bay leaves*
2 parsley sprigs	*2 parsley sprigs*
1 × 15 ml spoon/ 1 tablespoon lemon juice	*1 tablespoon lemon juice*
salt	*salt*
freshly ground black pepper	*freshly ground black pepper*
1.2 litres/2 pints water	*5 cups water*
175 g/6 oz small button mushrooms	*1½ cups small button mushrooms*
40 g/1½ oz butter	*3 tablespoons butter*
40 g/1½ oz flour	*⅓ cup flour*
150 ml/¼ pint single cream	*⅔ cup light cream*
2 egg yolks	*2 egg yolks*

Put the veal into a saucepan, then just cover with water. Bring to the boil, skimming the scum from the surface. Drain, rinse out the pan, then return the veal cubes to the pan. Add the onions, carrots, herbs, lemon juice and salt and pepper to taste, then pour over the water. Bring to the boil. Cover and simmer for 1 hour. Stir in the mushrooms, re-cover and simmer for a further 30 minutes, or until the veal is cooked. Remove the bay leaves and parsley. Transfer the meat and vegetables to a rigid container.

Boil the cooking liquid briskly until it has reduced to 600 ml/1 pint/2½ cups. Melt the butter in a saucepan and stir in the flour to make a smooth paste. Cook for 1 minute. Stir in the reduced stock and bring to the boil, stirring continuously. Simmer for 2 to 3 minutes. Combine the cream and egg yolks together in a small bowl. Gradually stir about 4 × 15 ml spoons/4 tablespoons of the sauce into the bowl mixture, beat well, then stir the mixture back into the sauce. Pour the sauce over the meat and vegetables.

To freeze: cool quickly, cover, label and freeze.
Storage life: up to 2 months
To thaw and serve: turn into a double saucepan or heatproof bowl set over a pan of simmering water and thaw over a very low heat. Simmer for about 45 minutes, or until the sauce is hot but not boiling.
Serves 4 to 6

Blanquette de veau

*Danish meatballs with onion sauce

METRIC/IMPERIAL	AMERICAN
350 g/12 oz minced pork	¾ lb ground pork
350 g/12 oz minced beef	¾ lb ground beef
175 g/6 oz fresh breadcrumbs	3 cups fresh breadcrumbs
1 onion, grated	1 onion, grated
salt	salt
freshly ground black pepper	freshly ground black pepper
1 × 2.5 ml spoon/ ½ teaspoon grated nutmeg	½ teaspoon grated nutmeg
1 × 15 ml spoon/ 1 tablespoon chopped parsley	1 tablespoon chopped parsley
1 egg, lightly beaten	1 egg, lightly beaten
oil for shallow frying	oil for shallow frying
Sauce:	**Sauce:**
50 g/2 oz butter	¼ cup butter
3 onions, chopped	3 onions, chopped
1 × 5 ml spoon/ 1 teaspoon sugar	1 teaspoon sugar
40 g/1½ oz flour	⅓ cup flour
600 ml/1 pint beef stock	2½ cups beef stock
1 × 15 ml spoon/ 1 tablespoon tomato purée	1 tablespoon tomato paste
dash of chilli sauce	dash of chili sauce
salt	salt
freshly ground black pepper	freshly ground black pepper

Put all the ingredients for the meat balls, except the oil, in a mixing bowl and mix well. With floured hands, shape the mixture into walnut-sized balls. Heat the oil in a large frying pan (skillet) and fry the balls for 10 to 12 minutes, or until they are cooked and golden brown. Drain on paper towels, then transfer to a rigid container.

To make the sauce, melt the butter in a saucepan and add the onions. Fry gently until they are soft. Stir in the sugar and flour to make a smooth paste. Cook for 1 minute. Stir in the stock and bring to the boil, stirring continuously. Simmer for 2 to 3 minutes. Stir in the remaining sauce ingredients and simmer for a further 2 minutes. Spoon the sauce over the meat balls.

To freeze: cool quickly, cover, label and freeze.
Storage life: up to 2 months
To thaw and serve: turn into a casserole and put, covered, into a preheated moderate oven (180°C/350°F, Gas Mark 4) for 45 minutes, stirring occasionally.
Serves 6

Chinese barbecued pork

METRIC/IMPERIAL	AMERICAN
0.5 kg/1 lb pork fillet	1 lb pork tenderloin
1 × 15 ml spoon/ 1 tablespoon medium sherry	1 tablespoon medium sherry
1 × 15 ml spoon/ 1 tablespoon soy sauce	1 tablespoon soy sauce
1 × 15 ml spoon/ 1 tablespoon sugar	1 tablespoon sugar
2 × 5 ml spoons/ 2 teaspoons salt	2 teaspoons salt
1 × 5 ml spoon/ 1 teaspoon freshly ground black pepper	1 teaspoon freshly ground black pepper

Cut the pork into strips about 10 cm × 2.5 cm/4 inches × 1 inch. Combine all the remaining ingredients together in a large bowl, then stir in the pork strips. Set aside for 1 hour, basting occasionally.
To freeze: turn into a polythene (plastic) bag, seal, label and freeze.
Storage life: up to 3 months
To thaw and serve: thaw for 4 hours at room temperature. Arrange the strips on the lined rack of a grill (broiler) pan. Grill (broil) for 6 minutes on each side, or until the strips are cooked.
Serves 4

Chinese barbecued chicken

METRIC/IMPERIAL	AMERICAN
dash of chilli sauce	dash of chili sauce
2 × 5 ml spoons/ 2 teaspoons medium sherry	2 teaspoons medium sherry
1 × 2.5 ml spoon/ ½ teaspoon caster sugar	½ teaspoon sugar
1 × 5 ml spoon/ 1 teaspoon freshly ground black pepper	1 teaspoon freshly ground black pepper
pinch of salt	pinch of salt
1 × 5 ml spoon/ 1 teaspoon soy sauce	1 teaspoon soy sauce
1 × 2.5 ml spoon/ ½ teaspoon sesame seeds	½ teaspoon sesame seeds
225 g/8 oz cooked chicken, cubed	½ lb cooked chicken, cubed
oil for deep frying	oil for deep frying

Mix all the ingredients together, except the chicken and oil. Stir in the chicken cubes and set aside for 30 minutes. Lightly grease six 15 cm/6 inch square pieces of heavy-duty foil. Divide the chicken between the foil pieces and wrap firmly to enclose it completely.
To freeze: seal, label and freeze.
Storage life: up to 2 months
To thaw and serve: deep fry the parcels, a few at a time, for 5 minutes. Drain and serve in the foil.
Serves 2 to 3

Chicken curry

*Chicken curry

METRIC/IMPERIAL	AMERICAN
4 × 15 ml spoons/ 4 tablespoons cooking oil	¼ cup cooking oil
4 large chicken pieces	4 large chicken pieces
2 onions, chopped	2 onions, chopped
25 g/1 oz flour	¼ cup flour
1 × 15 ml spoon/ 1 tablespoon curry powder	1 tablespoon curry powder
300 ml/½ pint chicken stock	1¼ cups chicken stock
1 × 15 ml spoon/ 1 tablespoon mango chutney	1 tablespoon mango chutney
1 × 15 ml spoon/ 1 tablespoon cherry jam	1 tablespoon cherry jam
salt	salt
freshly ground black pepper	freshly ground black pepper
1 dessert apple, cored and chopped	1 dessert apple, cored and chopped
2 × 15 ml spoons/ 2 tablespoons raisins	2 tablespoons raisins

Heat the oil in a saucepan and add the chicken pieces. Fry until they are browned all over, then transfer to a plate. Add the onions and fry gently until they are soft. Stir in the flour and curry powder to make a smooth paste. Cook for 1 minute. Stir in the stock and bring to the boil, stirring continuously. Simmer for 2 to 3 minutes. Stir in the chutney, jam and salt and pepper to taste. Return the chicken pieces to the pan and baste well. Cover and simmer for 45 minutes. Stir in the apple and raisins and simmer for a further 10 minutes, or until the chicken is cooked.

To freeze: cool quickly and turn into a rigid container. Cover, label and freeze.

Storage life: up to 2 months

To thaw and serve: turn into an ovenproof dish and put, covered, into a preheated moderate oven (160°C/325°F, Gas Mark 3) for 40 minutes, stirring occasionally. Serve with lemon wedges and separate side dishes.

Serves 4

Chicken pie

Chicken pie

METRIC/IMPERIAL
50 g/2 oz butter
100 g/4 oz mushrooms,
 sliced
2 carrots, sliced
25 g/1 oz flour
300 ml/½ pint milk
pinch of ground mace
salt
freshly ground black
 pepper
juice of ½ lemon
225 g/8 oz cooked
 chicken meat, cubed
100 g/4 oz cooked lean
 bacon, chopped
225 g/8 oz frozen puff
 pastry, thawed
1 egg, beaten

AMERICAN
¼ cup butter
1 cup sliced mushrooms
2 carrots, sliced
¼ cup flour
1¼ cups milk
pinch of ground mace
salt
freshly ground black
 pepper
juice of ½ lemon
½ lb cooked chicken meat,
 cubed
¼ lb cooked Canadian
 bacon, chopped
½ lb frozen puff pastry,
 thawed
1 egg, beaten

Melt half the butter in a frying pan (skillet) and add the mushrooms and carrots. Fry gently until they are soft. Using a slotted spoon, transfer the vegetables to a plate. Add the remaining butter to the pan and stir in the flour to make a smooth paste. Cook for 1 minute. Stir in the milk and bring to the boil, stirring continuously. Simmer for 2 to 3 minutes. Stir in the mace, salt and pepper to taste and lemon juice, then add the chicken, bacon and reserved vegetables. Simmer for 5 minutes. Set aside to cool.

Roll out the pastry dough on a lightly floured surface. Turn the chicken mixture into a medium freezer-proof pie dish (pan). Cover with the dough, using the trimmings to make decorations. Make a slit in the centre.

To freeze: open freeze. When frozen, put into a polythene (plastic) bag, seal, label and return to the freezer.

Storage life: up to 2 months

To thaw and serve: Brush the top of the pie with the beaten egg and put into a preheated hot oven (220°C/425°F, Gas Mark 7) for 25 to 30 minutes, or until the pastry is golden brown.

Serves 4

Chicken with tarragon

METRIC/IMPERIAL
1.75 kg/4 lb roasting
  chicken
juice and grated rind of 2
  large oranges
15 g/½ oz cornflour
300 ml/½ pint chicken
  stock
1 onion, chopped
1 × 15 ml spoon/
  1 tablespoon chopped
  tarragon
salt
freshly ground black
  pepper
150 ml/¼ pint sour cream

AMERICAN
4 lb roasting chicken
juice and grated rind of 2
  large oranges
2 tablespoons cornstarch
1¼ cups chicken stock
1 onion, chopped
1 tablespoon chopped
  tarragon
salt
freshly ground black
  pepper
⅔ cup sour cream

Roast the chicken in a preheated moderate oven (180°C/350°F, Gas Mark 4) for 1½ hours, or until it is cooked. Set aside until it is cool enough to handle. Skim the scum from the cooking juices and reserve the juices. Skin and bone the chicken and chop the meat into small chunks. Transfer the meat to a rigid container.

Pour the orange juice into a saucepan and heat until it is hot. Stir in the cornflour (cornstarch) to make a smooth paste. Cook for 1 minute. Stir in the rind, stock, reserved cooking juices and onion and bring to the boil, stirring continuously. Stir in the chopped tarragon and salt and pepper to taste and simmer for 2 to 3 minutes. Pour the sauce over the chicken.
To freeze: cool quickly, cover, label and freeze.
Storage life: up to 2 months
To thaw and serve: thaw, covered, overnight in the refrigerator. Turn into a saucepan and thaw over a very low heat. Bring the mixture to the boil, stirring continuously. Stir in the sour cream before serving.
Serves 4

*Chicken Kiev

METRIC/IMPERIAL
8 large chicken breasts,
  boned
225 g/8 oz butter, softened
3 garlic cloves, crushed
2 × 5 ml spoons/
  2 teaspoons chopped
  parsley
salt
freshly ground black
  pepper
40 g/1½ oz seasoned flour
2 eggs, beaten
175 g/6 oz dry
  breadcrumbs
oil for deep frying

AMERICAN
8 large chicken breasts,
  boned
1 cup butter, softened
3 garlic cloves, crushed
2 teaspoons chopped
  parsley
salt
freshly ground black
  pepper
⅓ cup seasoned flour
2 eggs, beaten
1½ cups dry breadcrumbs
oil for deep frying

Put the boned chicken breasts between two pieces of dampened greaseproof (waxed) paper. Pound until they are about 5 mm/¼ inch thick.

Beat the butter, garlic, parsley, salt and pepper together until they are thoroughly blended. Shape the mixture into 8 sausage shapes, cover and chill in the refrigerator until they are firm.

Lay the breasts out flat and place one butter shape in the centre of each one. Roll up, parcel style, to enclose the filling completely. Dip the rolls, one by one, in the flour, then the eggs and finally in the breadcrumbs, making sure they are all thoroughly coated.
To freeze: open freeze. When frozen, wrap in heavy-duty foil, seal, label and return to the freezer.
Storage life: up to 3 months
To thaw and serve: thaw for 4 hours in the refrigerator, then deep fry in hot oil for 10 minutes, or until they are crisp and golden brown. Drain on paper towels before serving.
Serves 8

*Chilli con carne

METRIC/IMPERIAL
3 × 15 ml spoons/
  3 tablespoons cooking oil
1 onion, chopped
1 garlic clove, crushed
1 small green pepper,
  deseeded and chopped
0.5 kg/1 lb minced beef
1 × 15 ml spoon/
  1 tablespoon mild chilli
  powder
1 × 2.5 ml spoon/
  ½ teaspoon ground cumin
2 × 15 ml spoons
  2 tablespoons tomato
  purée
1 × 225 g/8 oz can
  tomatoes
1 × 400 g/14 oz can red
  kidney beans, drained

AMERICAN
3 tablespoons cooking oil
1 onion, chopped
1 garlic clove, crushed
1 small green pepper,
  deseeded and chopped
1 lb ground beef
1 tablespoon mild chili
  powder
½ teaspoon ground cumin
2 tablespoons tomato
  paste
1 × ½ lb can tomatoes
1 × 14 oz can red
  kidney beans, drained

Heat the oil in a saucepan and add the onion, garlic and pepper. Fry gently until they are soft. Add the minced (ground) beef and fry until it loses its pinkness. Stir in all the remaining ingredients and bring to the boil. Cover and simmer for 1¼ hours.
To freeze: cool quickly and turn into a rigid container. Cover, label and freeze.
Storage life: up to 2 months
To thaw and serve: thaw overnight in the refrigerator. Turn into a saucepan and bring slowly to the boil, stirring occasionally. Simmer for 5 minutes.
Serves 4

Swiss steak

METRIC/IMPERIAL
0.75 kg/1½ lb braising
  steak, cut into eight
  2.5 cm/1 inch thick pieces
25 g/1 oz seasoned flour
4 × 15 ml spoons/
  4 tablespoons cooking oil
2 onions, chopped
1 garlic clove, crushed
2 celery sticks, chopped
1 × 225 g/8 oz can
  tomatoes
1 × 15 ml spoon/
  1 tablespoon tomato
  purée
1 × 2.5 ml spoon/
  ½ teaspoon
  Worcestershire sauce
150 ml/¼ pint beef stock
salt
freshly ground black
  pepper

AMERICAN
1½ lb chuck steak, cut into
  eight 1 inch thick pieces
¼ cup seasoned flour
¼ cup cooking oil
2 onions, chopped
1 garlic clove, crushed
2 celery stalks, chopped
1 × ½ lb can tomatoes
1 tablespoon tomato paste
½ teaspoon
  Worcestershire sauce
⅔ cup beef stock
salt
freshly ground black
  pepper

Coat the meat in the flour. Heat the oil in a deep frying pan (skillet) and add the meat. Fry until it is browned on both sides. Transfer to a casserole.

Add the onions, garlic and celery to the pan and fry until they are soft. Stir in the tomatoes, tomato purée (paste), Worcestershire sauce, stock and salt and pepper to taste. Bring to the boil, stirring continuously. Spoon over the meat pieces and put the dish into a preheated moderate oven (160°C/325°F, Gas Mark 3). Cook for 2½ hours, or until the meat is cooked.
To freeze: cool quickly and turn into a rigid foil container. Cover, label and freeze.
Storage life: up to 2 months
To thaw and serve: put, covered, into a preheated moderate oven (160°C/325°F, Gas Mark 3) for 45 minutes, stirring occasionally.
Serves 4

*Duckling à l'orange

METRIC/IMPERIAL
1.75 kg/4 lb duckling
salt
freshly ground black
  pepper
coarsely grated rind and
  juice of 2 oranges
coarsely grated rind and
  juice of 1 lemon
1 × 15 ml spoon/
  1 tablespoon flour
2 × 15 ml spoons/
  2 tablespoons red wine
250 ml/8 fl oz stock
  (made from the duck
  giblets)
1 × 15 ml spoon/
  1 tablespoon redcurrant
  jelly

AMERICAN
4 lb duckling
salt
freshly ground black
  pepper
coarsely grated rind and
  juice of 2 oranges
coarsely grated rind and
  juice of 1 lemon
1 tablespoon flour
2 tablespoons red wine
1 cup stock (made from
  the duck giblets)
1 tablespoon redcurrant
  jelly

Rub the duckling, inside and outside, with salt and pepper. Prick the skin all over and put the duckling on the rack in a roasting pan. Put the pan into a preheated moderate oven (180°C/350°F, Gas Mark 4) and roast for 2 hours, or until the duckling is cooked. Remove from the oven and carve the duckling into serving pieces. Transfer to a large foil container.

Reserve 1 × 15 ml spoon/1 tablespoon of the cooking juices. Blanch the orange and lemon rinds in boiling water for 3 minutes, then drain. Pour the reserved cooking liquid into a saucepan and stir in the flour to make a smooth paste. Cook for 1 minute. Stir in the orange and lemon rind and juice, the wine, stock and jelly, and bring to the boil, stirring continuously. Simmer for 2 to 3 minutes. Pour the sauce over the duck.
To freeze: cool quickly, cover, label and freeze.
Storage life: up to 2 months
To thaw and serve: thaw, covered, overnight in the refrigerator. Put, covered, into a preheated moderately hot oven (200°C/400°F, Gas Mark 6) for 35 minutes.
Serves 4

Game casserole

METRIC/IMPERIAL
3 mature grouse, plucked
  and drawn
25 g/1 oz butter
1 large onion, chopped
2 carrots, chopped
1 small turnip, diced
1 celery stick, chopped
3 rashers bacon, chopped
150 ml/¼ pint red wine
300 ml/½ pint beef stock
1 × 15 ml spoon/
  1 tablespoon redcurrant
  jelly
juice of ½ lemon
salt
freshly ground black
  pepper

AMERICAN
3 mature grouse, plucked
  and drawn
2 tablespoons butter
1 large onion, chopped
2 carrots, chopped
1 small turnip, diced
1 celery stalk, chopped
3 slices Canadian bacon,
  chopped
⅔ cup red wine
1¼ cups beef stock
1 tablespoon redcurrant
  jelly
juice of ½ lemon
salt
freshly ground black
  pepper

Cut the grouse in half. Melt the butter in a saucepan and add the grouse halves. Fry until they are browned all over. Transfer to a medium casserole. Add the onion, carrots, turnip and celery to the pan and fry gently until they are soft. Add the bacon and fry until golden brown. Stir in all the remaining ingredients and bring to the boil, stirring continuously. Pour over the grouse. Cover and put the casserole into a preheated cool oven (150°C/300°F, Gas Mark 2). Cook for 2½ hours, or until the grouse is cooked.
To freeze: cool quickly and turn into a rigid container or polythene (plastic) bag. Cover or seal, label and freeze.
Storage life: up to 6 weeks
To thaw and serve: turn into a casserole and put into a preheated moderate oven (160°C/325°F, Gas Mark 3) for 40 minutes, stirring occasionally.
Serves 6

*Hamburgers

METRIC/IMPERIAL
0.5 kg/1 lb minced beef
50 g/2 oz fresh
  breadcrumbs
1 egg, lightly beaten
2 × 15 ml spoons/
  2 tablespoons milk
1 small onion, grated
2 × 5 ml spoons/
  2 teaspoons chopped
  parsley
1 × 2.5 ml spoon/
  ½ teaspoon mustard
salt
freshly ground black
  pepper
oil for shallow frying

AMERICAN
1 lb ground beef
1 cup fresh breadcrumbs
1 egg, lightly beaten
2 tablespoons milk
1 small onion, grated
2 teaspoons chopped
  parsley
½ teaspoon mustard
salt
freshly ground black
  pepper
oil for shallow frying

Put all the ingredients, except the oil, in a large mixing bowl and mix well. With floured hands, divide the mixture into 8 portions, then shape each portion into a flat, thick round.

To freeze: open freeze on a baking sheet. When frozen, wrap each hamburger individually in heavy-duty foil. Put them into a polythene (plastic) bag, seal, label and return to the freezer.

Storage life: up to 2 months

To thaw and serve: fry the frozen hamburgers in oil for 6 to 8 minutes on each side. Serve with fresh baps, tomato slices and fried onion rings.
Serves 4 to 8

Liver and onions

METRIC/IMPERIAL
25 g/1 oz butter
4 rashers lean bacon,
  chopped
2 large onions, chopped
25 g/1 oz flour
300 ml/½ pint beef stock
salt
freshly ground black
  pepper
0.5 kg/1 lb lambs' liver,
  thinly sliced
1 × 15 ml spoon/
  1 tablespoon chopped
  parsley

AMERICAN
2 tablespoons butter
4 slices Canadian bacon,
  chopped
2 large onions, chopped
¼ cup flour
1¼ cups beef stock
salt
freshly ground black
  pepper
1 lb lamb liver, thinly
  sliced
1 tablespoon chopped
  parsley

Melt the butter in a saucepan and add the bacon. Fry until it is golden brown, then transfer to a plate. Add the onions and fry gently until they are soft. Stir in the flour to make a smooth paste. Cook for 1 minute. Stir in the stock and bring to the boil, stirring continuously. Add the salt and pepper to taste. Add the liver and reserved bacon to the pan, cover and simmer for 15 minutes.

To freeze: cool quickly and turn into a polythene (plastic) bag. Seal, label and freeze.

Storage life: up to 6 weeks

To thaw and serve: put into a double boiler or heat-proof bowl set over a pan of simmering water. Thaw over a very low heat for 15 minutes.
Serves 4

Hamburger

*Hungarian pork

METRIC/IMPERIAL	AMERICAN
25 g/1 oz butter	2 tablespoons butter
1 kg/2 lb pork fillet, cubed	2 lb pork tenderloin, cubed
1 onion, chopped	1 onion, chopped
1 garlic clove, crushed	1 garlic clove, crushed
1 × 15 ml spoon/ 1 tablespoon paprika	1 tablespoon paprika
1 × 15 ml spoon/ 1 tablespoon flour	1 tablespoon flour
300 ml/½ pint beef stock	1¼ cups beef stock
5 × 15 ml spoons/ 5 tablespoons sherry	⅓ cup sherry
2 × 15 ml spoons/ 2 tablespoons tomato purée	2 tablespoons tomato paste
salt	salt
freshly ground black pepper	freshly ground black pepper
175 g/6 oz small button mushrooms	1½ cups small button mushrooms
150 ml/¼ pint sour cream	⅔ cup sour cream

Melt the butter in a saucepan and add the pork cubes. Fry until they are browned all over. Transfer the cubes to a plate. Add the onion, garlic and paprika and fry gently until the onion is soft. Stir in the flour to make a smooth paste. Cook for 1 minute. Stir in the stock, sherry, tomato purée (paste) and salt and pepper to taste and bring to the boil. Return the meat to the pan, cover and simmer for 1 hour, or until the pork is cooked. Stir in the mushrooms and simmer for a further 5 minutes.

To freeze: cool quickly and turn into a rigid foil container. Cover, label and freeze.

Storage life: up to 2 months

To thaw and serve: put, covered, into a preheated moderate oven (160°C/325°F, Gas Mark 3) for 40 minutes. Stir in the sour cream before serving.

Serves 4

Hungarian pork

Hare in Madeira sauce

METRIC/IMPERIAL	AMERICAN
1 hare, cut into serving pieces	1 hare, cut into serving pieces
50 g/2 oz seasoned flour	½ cup seasoned flour
175 g/6 oz butter	¾ cup butter
225 g/8 oz small mushrooms	2 cups small mushrooms
300 ml/½ pint Madeira	1¼ cups Madeira
1 × 5 ml spoon/ 1 teaspoon rubbed sage	1 teaspoon rubbed sage
salt	salt
freshly ground black pepper	freshly ground black pepper

Coat the hare pieces in the flour. Melt half the butter in a frying pan (skillet) and add the hare pieces. Fry until they are browned all over. Transfer to a casserole.

Melt the remaining butter in the pan and add the mushrooms. Fry gently until they are soft. Stir in the Madeira, sage and salt and pepper to taste, and bring to the boil. Pour the mixture over the hare pieces. Cover the casserole and put into a preheated moderately hot oven (190°C/375°F, Gas Mark 5). Cook for 1 to 1½ hours, or until the hare is cooked.

To freeze: cool quickly and turn into a rigid container. Cover, label and freeze.

Storage life: up to 2 months

To thaw and serve: turn into a casserole and put, covered, into a preheated moderate oven (180°C/ 350°F, Gas Mark 4) for 45 minutes.

Serves 6

Individual steak and kidney pies

METRIC/IMPERIAL
0.75 kg/1½ lb braising
  steak, cubed
2 lamb's kidneys, trimmed
  and chopped
25 g/1 oz seasoned flour
3 × 15 ml spoons/
  3 tablespoons cooking oil
2 small onions, chopped
1 garlic clove, crushed
300 ml/½ pint beef stock
salt
freshly ground black
  pepper
350 g/12 oz frozen
  shortcrust pastry, thawed
1 egg, lightly beaten

AMERICAN
1½ lb chuck steak, cubed
2 lamb kidneys, trimmed
  and chopped
¼ cup seasoned flour
3 tablespoons cooking oil
2 small onions, chopped
1 garlic clove, crushed
1¼ cups beef stock
salt
freshly ground black
  pepper
¾ lb frozen basic pie
  dough, thawed
1 egg, lightly beaten

Coat the steak and kidney in the seasoned flour. Heat the oil in a saucepan and add the onions and garlic. Fry gently until they are soft. Add the steak and kidney and fry until they are browned all over. Stir in the stock and salt and pepper and bring to the boil. Cover and simmer for 2 hours, or until the meat is cooked. Set aside to cool.

Roll out two-thirds of the pastry dough on a lightly floured surface and use to line 6 well-greased 10 cm/4 inch patty tins (pans). Divide the meat mixture between the tins (pans). Roll out the remaining pastry dough and cut out 6 circles for lids. Dampen the edges of the dough, then cover and crimp to seal. Make a slit in the centre of each pie. Brush with the beaten egg. Put the tins (pans) into a preheated moderately hot oven (200°C/400°F, Gas Mark 6) and bake for 30 minutes, or until the pastry is golden brown.

To freeze: cool quickly and wrap individually in heavy-duty foil. Pack them into a polythene (plastic) bag, seal, label and freeze.

Storage life: up to 1 month

To thaw and serve: thaw for 2 to 3 hours at room temperature, then put into a preheated moderately hot oven (200°C/400°F, Gas Mark 6) for 20 minutes. Serves 6

Individual steak and kidney pie

Some of the ingredients for Jugged steak

Jugged steak

METRIC/IMPERIAL	AMERICAN
40 g/1½ oz butter	3 tablespoons butter
0.75 kg/1½ lb braising steak, cubed	1½ lb chuck steak, cubed
2 small onions, each stuck with 2 cloves	2 small onions, each stuck with 2 cloves
2 celery sticks, sliced	2 celery stalks, sliced
10 peppercorns	10 peppercorns
thinly pared rind of 1 lemon	thinly pared rind of 1 lemon
pinch of cayenne	pinch of cayenne
1 mace blade	1 mace blade
2 thyme sprigs	2 thyme sprigs
2 parsley sprigs	2 parsley sprigs
salt	salt
freshly ground black pepper	freshly ground black pepper
600 ml/1 pint water	2½ cups water
25 g/1 oz flour	¼ cup flour
150 ml/¼ pint port	⅔ cup port
1.5 × 15 ml spoons/ 1½ tablespoons redcurrant jelly	1½ tablespoons redcurrant jelly

Melt the butter in a frying pan (skillet) and add the beef cubes. Fry until they are browned all over, then transfer to a flameproof casserole. Add the onions, celery, peppercorns, lemon rind, cayenne, mace, herbs, salt and pepper and water to the casserole and bring to the boil. Cover and put into a preheated moderate oven (160°C/325°F, Gas Mark 3). Cook for 2 hours, or until the meat is cooked. Transfer the beef cubes to a rigid container.

Strain the cooking liquid into a saucepan. Mix the flour with a little cooking liquid, then stir the paste into the remaining cooking liquid. Bring to the boil, stirring continuously, then simmer for 2 to 3 minutes, or until the sauce has thickened. Stir in the port and redcurrant jelly. Pour the sauce over the meat cubes.

To freeze: cool quickly, cover, label and freeze.

Storage life: up to 2 months

To thaw and serve: turn into a casserole and put, covered, into a preheated moderate oven (160°C/ 325°F, Gas Mark 3) for 45 minutes, stirring occasionally.

Serves 4

Kashmir beef

METRIC/IMPERIAL	AMERICAN
6 × 15 ml spoons/ 6 tablespoons ghee or butter	6 tablespoons ghee or butter
2 medium onions, chopped	2 medium onions, chopped
2 garlic cloves, crushed	2 garlic cloves, crushed
5 cm/2 inch piece root ginger, peeled and chopped	2 inch piece ginger root, peeled and chopped
2 carrots, grated	2 carrots, grated
1 small dessert apple, peeled, cored and sliced	1 small dessert apple, peeled, cored and sliced
1 × 225 g/8 oz can pineapple chunks, with juice reserved	1 × ½ lb can pineapple chunks, with juice reserved
1 × 15 ml spoon/ 1 tablespoon hot curry powder	1 tablespoon hot curry powder
1 × 15 ml spoon/ 1 tablespoon flour	1 tablespoon flour
300 ml/½ pint beef stock	1¼ cups beef stock
2 × 15 ml spoons/ 2 tablespoons desiccated coconut	2 tablespoons shredded coconut
2 × 15 ml spoons/ 2 tablespoons sultanas	2 tablespoons seedless white raisins
1 × 15 ml spoon/ 1 tablespoon sweet chutney	1 tablespoon sweet chutney
0.75 kg/1½ lb braising steak, cubed	1½ lb chuck steak, cubed
1 × 5 ml spoon/ 1 teaspoon sugar	1 teaspoon sugar
1 × 5 ml spoon/ 1 teaspoon vinegar	1 teaspoon vinegar
salt	salt
freshly ground black pepper	freshly ground black pepper

Melt half the ghee or butter in a large saucepan and add the onions, garlic and ginger. Fry gently until they are soft. Stir in the carrots, apple and pineapple chunks, and cook for 1 minute. Stir in the curry powder and flour to make a smooth paste. Cook for 1 minute. Stir in the stock and pineapple can juice and bring to the boil, stirring continuously. Simmer for 2 to 3 minutes. Stir in the coconut, sultanas (raisins) and chutney and simmer for 10 minutes.

Melt the remaining ghee or butter in a frying pan (skillet) and add the beef cubes. Fry until they are browned all over. Stir into the sauce mixture, with all the remaining ingredients. Cover and simmer for 2 hours, or until the beef is cooked.

To freeze: cool quickly and turn into a rigid container. Cover, label and freeze.

Storage life: up to 2 months

To thaw and serve: turn into a casserole and put, covered, into a preheated moderate oven (180°C/ 350°F, Gas Mark 4) for 40 minutes, stirring occasionally.

Serves 4

*Meat loaf

METRIC/IMPERIAL	AMERICAN
0.5 kg/1 lb pork sausage meat	1 lb pork sausage meat
0.5 kg/1 lb minced beef	1 lb ground beef
350 g/12 oz minced pigs' liver	¾ lb ground pork liver
1 medium onion, grated	1 medium onion, grated
1 garlic clove, crushed	1 garlic clove, crushed
1 × 5 ml spoon/1 teaspoon dried thyme	1 teaspoon dried thyme
1 × 2.5 ml spoon/ ½ teaspoon rubbed sage	½ teaspoon rubbed sage
salt	salt
freshly ground black pepper	freshly ground black pepper
1 egg, lightly beaten	1 egg, lightly beaten
2 × 15 ml spoons/ 2 tablespoons red wine	2 tablespoons red wine

Put all the ingredients into a mixing bowl and blend well. Turn into a well-greased 1 kg/2 lb loaf tin (pan). Stand in a roasting pan and pour in enough boiling water to come half-way up the sides. Bake in a pre-heated moderate oven (180°C/350°F, Gas Mark 3) for 1½ hours, or until the loaf shrinks from the edge of the tin.

To freeze: cool quickly, turn out of the tin and wrap in heavy-duty foil. Put in a polythene (plastic) bag, seal, label and freeze.

Storage life: up to 2 months

To thaw and serve: thaw overnight in the refrigerator. Cut into thick slices before serving.

Serves 4 to 6

Kidneys in red wine

METRIC/IMPERIAL	AMERICAN
50 g/2 oz butter	¼ cup butter
8 lambs' kidneys, trimmed and halved	8 lamb kidneys, trimmed and halved
2 small onions, sliced	2 small onions, sliced
2 small carrots, sliced	2 small carrots, sliced
15 g/½ oz flour	2 tablespoons flour
300 ml/½ pint red wine	1¼ cups red wine
300 ml/½ pint beef stock	1¼ cups beef stock
1 × 15 ml spoon/ 1 tablespoon tomato purée	1 tablespoon tomato paste
1 thyme sprig	1 thyme sprig
1 bouquet garni	1 bouquet garni
225 g/8 oz mushrooms, sliced	2 cups sliced mushrooms
1 × 15 ml spoon/ 1 tablespoon chopped parsley to garnish	1 tablespoon chopped parsley to garnish

Melt the butter in a saucepan and add the kidneys. Fry until they are browned all over, then transfer them to a plate. Add the onions and carrots and fry gently until they are soft. Stir in the flour to make a smooth paste. Cook for 1 minute. Stir in the wine, stock and tomato purée (paste) and bring to the boil. Return the kidneys to the pan with the herbs. Cover and simmer for 15 minutes. Stir in the mushrooms, re-cover and simmer for a further 5 minutes, or until the kidneys are cooked. Remove the herbs, then turn the mixture into a shallow ovenproof dish.

To freeze: cool quickly, cover and freeze until solid. Turn out of the dish and put in a polythene (plastic) bag. Seal, label and return to the freezer.

Storage life: up to 2 months

To thaw and serve: turn into an ovenproof dish and put into a preheated moderately hot oven (190°C/ 375°F, Gas Mark 5) for 20 minutes. Garnish with the chopped parsley before serving.

Serves 4

*Lamb fricassée

METRIC/IMPERIAL	AMERICAN
0.75 kg/1½ lb lean lamb, cubed	1½ lb lean lamb, cubed
3 small onions, halved	3 small onions, halved
2 large carrots, quartered	2 large carrots, quartered
2 celery sticks, chopped	2 celery stalks, chopped
2 bay leaves	2 bay leaves
1 bouquet garni	1 bouquet garni
salt	salt
freshly ground black pepper	freshly ground black pepper
175 g/6 oz small button mushrooms, halved	1½ cups halved, small button mushrooms
40 g/1½ oz butter	3 tablespoons butter
40 g/1½ oz flour	⅓ cup flour
150 ml/¼ pint single cream	⅔ cup light cream

Put the lamb into a saucepan, then just cover with water. Bring to the boil, skimming the scum from the surface. Drain, rinse out the pan, then return the lamb cubes to the pan. Add the onions, carrots, celery, herbs and salt and pepper to taste. Pour over 1.2 litres/ 2 pints/5 cups of water and bring to the boil. Cover and simmer for 45 minutes. Stir in the mushrooms, re-cover and simmer for a further 30 minutes, or until the lamb is cooked.

Remove the bay leaves and bouquet garni, then transfer the meat and vegetables to a rigid container. Boil the cooking liquid briskly until it has reduced to 600 ml/1 pint/2½ cups. Melt the butter in a saucepan and stir in the flour to make a smooth paste. Cook for 1 minute. Stir in the reduced cooking liquid and bring to the boil, stirring continuously. Simmer for 2 to 3 minutes. Spoon over the meat and vegetables.

To freeze: cool quickly, cover, label and freeze.

Storage life: up to 2 months

To thaw and serve: turn into a saucepan and thaw over a very low heat. Bring the mixture to the boil. Stir in the cream just before serving.

Serves 4

Lancashire hot pot

Lancashire hot pot

METRIC/IMPERIAL
1 kg/2 lb lamb chops
25 g/1 oz seasoned flour
3 onions, sliced
2 lamb's kidneys,
  trimmed and quartered
175 g/6 oz mushrooms,
  sliced
salt
freshly ground black
  pepper
0.75 kg/1½ lb potatoes,
  sliced
450 ml/¾ pint beef stock
15 g/½ oz butter, cut into
  small pieces

AMERICAN
2 lb lamb chops
¼ cup seasoned flour
3 onions, sliced
2 lamb's kidneys,
  trimmed and quartered
1½ cups sliced mushrooms
salt
freshly ground black
  pepper
1½ lb potatoes, sliced
2 cups beef stock
1 tablespoon butter, cut
  into small pieces

Coat the chops in the flour. Arrange the chops, onions, kidneys and mushrooms in a deep casserole and sprinkle over the salt and pepper. Arrange the potato slices over the mixture to cover it completely. Pour over the stock and scatter over the butter. Put the dish into a preheated moderate oven (180°C/350°F, Gas Mark 4) and cook for 2 hours.
To freeze: cool quickly and turn into a rigid container. Cover, label and freeze.
Storage life: up to 6 weeks
To thaw and serve: turn into a casserole, with the potatoes on top, and put into a preheated moderate oven (180°C/350°F, Gas Mark 4) for 45 minutes. Uncover the dish for the last 30 minutes, to brown the potatoes.
Serves 4

Lasagne

METRIC/IMPERIAL	AMERICAN
Bolognese sauce:	**Bolognese sauce:**
4 × 15 ml spoons/ 4 tablespoons vegetable oil	¼ cup vegetable oil
2 onions, chopped	2 onions, chopped
2 garlic cloves, crushed	2 garlic cloves, crushed
2 celery sticks, chopped	2 celery stalks, chopped
0.5 kg/1 lb minced beef	1 lb ground beef
1 × 400 g/14 oz can tomatoes	1 × 14 oz can tomatoes
3 × 15 ml spoons/ 3 tablespoons tomato purée	3 tablespoons tomato paste
100 g/4 oz mushrooms	1 cup mushrooms
1 × 5 ml spoon/ 1 teaspoon grated lemon rind	1 teaspoon grated lemon rind
120 ml/4 fl oz red wine	½ cup red wine
salt	salt
freshly ground black pepper	freshly ground black pepper
2 × 5 ml spoons/ 2 teaspoons dried oregano	2 teaspoons dried oregano
350 ml/12 fl oz béchamel sauce (see page 32)	1½ cups béchamel sauce (see page 32)
Pasta:	**Pasta:**
2 × 5 ml spoons/ 2 teaspoons cooking oil	2 teaspoons cooking oil
2 × 5 ml spoons/ 2 teaspoons salt	2 teaspoons salt
175 g/6 oz lasagne	6 oz lasagne
100 g/4 oz Gruyère cheese, grated	1 cup grated Swiss cheese
50 g/2 oz grated Parmesan cheese	½ cup grated Parmesan cheese

To make the Bolognese sauce, heat the oil in a saucepan and add the onions, garlic and celery. Fry gently until they are soft. Add the minced (ground) beef and fry until it loses its pinkness.

Stir in the canned tomatoes, tomato purée (paste), mushrooms, lemon rind, red wine, salt and pepper to taste and the oregano and bring to the boil. Cover and simmer for 1 hour, stirring occasionally.

Meanwhile, three-quarters fill a large saucepan with water and add the oil and salt. Bring to the boil. Cook the lasagne, a few sheets at a time, in the water for about 10 minutes, or until just tender. To assemble the lasagne, line a large ovenproof baking dish with foil. Cover the bottom of the dish with a layer of pasta and top with a layer of half the Bolognese sauce. Cover with pasta, then add a layer of half the béchamel sauce, sprinkled with grated Gruyère (Swiss) cheese. Continue in this way until the ingredients are used up, ending with a layer of béchamel sauce sprinkled with the remaining grated Gruyère and Parmesan.

To freeze: cool quickly, then open freeze. When frozen, wrap completely in heavy-duty foil, then put in a polythene (plastic) bag, seal, label and freeze.

Storage life: up to 2 months

To thaw and serve: put, uncovered, into a preheated moderately hot oven (190°C/375°F, Gas Mark 5) for 1 hour.

Serves 6

Moussaka

METRIC/IMPERIAL	AMERICAN
1 kg/2 lb aubergines	2 lb eggplants
1 × 15 ml spoon/ 1 tablespoon salt	1 tablespoon salt
120 ml/4 fl oz cooking oil	½ cup cooking oil
2 onions, chopped	2 onions, chopped
2 garlic cloves, crushed	2 garlic cloves, crushed
0.5 kg/1 lb minced lamb or beef	1 lb ground lamb or beef
50 g/2 oz flour	½ cup flour
1 × 400 g/14 oz can tomatoes	1 × 14 oz can tomatoes
2 × 15 ml spoons/ 2 tablespoons tomato purée	2 tablespoons tomato paste
1 × 5 ml spoon/1 teaspoon dried rosemary	1 teaspoon dried rosemary
salt	salt
freshly ground black pepper	freshly ground black pepper
Sauce:	**Sauce:**
25 g/1 oz butter	2 tablespoons butter
300 ml/½ pint milk	1¼ cups milk
100 g/4 oz Cheddar cheese, grated	1 cup grated Cheddar cheese
salt	salt
freshly ground black pepper	freshly ground black pepper

Slice the aubergines (eggplants) and sprinkle over the salt. Set aside to dégorge for 30 minutes. Wipe dry with paper towels.

Heat 5 × 15 ml spoons/5 tablespoons/⅓ cup of the oil in a frying pan (skillet) and add the aubergine (eggplant) slices. Fry gently until they are browned all over. Set aside to drain on paper towels. Heat the remaining oil in a saucepan and add the onions and garlic. Fry gently until they are soft. Stir in the meat and fry until it loses its pinkness. Stir in half the flour, the tomatoes, tomato purée (paste), rosemary, salt and pepper to taste and bring to the boil. Cover and simmer for 20 minutes.

Arrange a third of the aubergine (eggplant) slices on the bottom of a fairly deep ovenproof dish. Cover with half the meat mixture. Continue layering, ending with a layer of aubergine (eggplant) slices.

To make the sauce, melt the butter in a saucepan and stir in the remaining flour to make a smooth paste. Cook for 1 minute. Stir in the milk and bring to the boil, stirring continuously. Stir in three-quarters of the grated cheese and salt and pepper to taste, until the cheese melts. Spoon the sauce over the meat and aubergine (eggplant) mixture, to cover it completely. Sprinkle over the remaining cheese.

To freeze: cool quickly, then open freeze. When frozen, remove from the dish and carefully turn into a polythene (plastic) bag. Seal, label and return to freezer.

Storage life: up to 6 weeks

To thaw and serve: carefully return to an ovenproof dish (topping uppermost) and put into a preheated moderately hot oven (200°C/400°F, Gas Mark 6) for 1 hour.

Serves 4

Moussaka

Normandy pork

Normandy pork

METRIC/IMPERIAL
25 g/1 oz butter
4 loin pork chops
2 onions, chopped
1 garlic clove, crushed
250 ml/8 fl oz dry white
  wine
1 × 15 ml spoon/
  1 tablespoon brandy
1 × 2.5 ml spoon/
  ½ teaspoon rubbed sage
2 dessert apples, peeled,
  cored and chopped
salt
freshly ground black
  pepper
1 × 15 ml spoon/
  1 tablespoon olive oil

AMERICAN
2 tablespoons butter
4 loin pork chops
2 onions, chopped
1 garlic clove, crushed
1 cup dry white wine
1 tablespoon brandy
½ teaspoon rubbed sage
2 dessert apples, peeled,
  cored and chopped
salt
freshly ground black
  pepper
1 tablespoon olive oil

Melt the butter in a frying pan (skillet) and add the chops. Fry until they are browned on both sides. Transfer to a casserole. Add the onions and garlic to the frying pan (skillet) and fry until they are soft. Stir in the wine, brandy, sage, apples and salt and pepper to taste. Bring to the boil. Simmer for 2 to 3 minutes. Spoon the sauce over and around the chops, arranging the chops so that they are above the sauce. Brush the exposed, fatty areas with the olive oil. Put the dish into a preheated moderate oven (180°C/350°F, Gas Mark 4) and bake for 45 minutes, or until the pork is cooked and the fat is crisp.

To freeze: cool quickly and turn into a rigid foil container. Cover, label and freeze.

Storage life: up to 2 months

To thaw and serve: put, covered, into a preheated moderate oven (180°C/350°F, Gas Mark 4) for 40 minutes.

Serves 4

*Mediterranean veal

METRIC/IMPERIAL	AMERICAN
4 × 15 ml spoons/ 4 tablespoons cooking oil	¼ cup cooking oil
1 kg/2 lb stewing veal, cubed	2 lb stewing veal, cubed
1 large onion, chopped	1 large onion, chopped
2 garlic cloves, crushed	2 garlic cloves, crushed
1 green pepper, deseeded and chopped	1 green pepper, deseeded and chopped
1 red pepper, deseeded and chopped	1 red pepper, deseeded and chopped
1 × 400 g/14 oz can tomatoes	1 × 14 oz can tomatoes
2 × 15 ml spoons/ 2 tablespoons tomato purée	2 tablespoons tomato paste
120 ml/4 fl oz dry white wine	½ cup dry white wine
2 × 5 ml spoons/ 2 teaspoons grated orange rind	2 teaspoons grated orange rind
1 × 5 ml spoon/1 teaspoon dried basil	1 teaspoon dried basil
salt	salt
freshly ground black pepper	freshly ground black pepper
black olives to garnish	black olives to garnish

Heat the oil in a saucepan and add the veal cubes. Fry until they are browned all over. Transfer to a plate. Add the onion, garlic and peppers to the pan and fry until they are soft. Stir in all the remaining ingredients, except the olives, and bring to the boil, stirring continuously. Cover and simmer for 1½ hours, or until the meat is cooked.

To freeze: cool quickly and turn into a rigid container. Cover, label and freeze.

Storage life: up to 2 months

To thaw and serve: turn into a saucepan and thaw over a very low heat. Simmer for 20 minutes. Garnish with black olives before serving.

Serves 6

*Oxtail casserole

METRIC/IMPERIAL	AMERICAN
1.5 kg/3 lb oxtail, sawn into 7.5 cm/3 inch pieces	3 lb oxtail, sawn into 3 inch pieces
50 g/2 oz seasoned flour	½ cup seasoned flour
50 g/2 oz butter	¼ cup butter
2 onions, chopped	2 onions, chopped
2 carrots, chopped	2 carrots, chopped
2 celery sticks, chopped	2 celery stalks, chopped
450 ml/¾ pint beef stock	2 cups beef stock
1 × 5 ml spoon/1 teaspoon dried thyme	1 teaspoon dried thyme
2 bay leaves	2 bay leaves
juice of 1 lemon	juice of 1 lemon

Coat the oxtail pieces in the flour. Melt the butter in a saucepan and add the oxtail pieces. Fry until they are browned all over, then transfer them to a casserole.

Add the onions, carrots and celery to the pan and fry gently until they are soft. Stir in any remaining flour to make a smooth paste. Cook for 1 minute. Stir in all the remaining ingredients and bring to the boil, stirring continuously. Pour over the oxtail. Cover and put the casserole into a preheated moderately hot oven (190°C/375°F, Gas Mark 5). Cook for 30 minutes, then reduce the temperature to cool (150°C/300°F, Gas Mark 2) and cook for a further 2 hours, or until the oxtail is cooked.

To freeze: cool quickly, remove any excess fat and turn into a rigid foil container. Cover, label and freeze.

Storage life: up to 2 months

To thaw and serve: thaw, covered, overnight in the refrigerator. Put, covered, into a preheated moderate oven (160°C/325°F, Gas Mark 3) for 1 hour.

Serves 4

Pheasant in rich cream sauce

METRIC/IMPERIAL	AMERICAN
25 g/1 oz butter	2 tablespoons butter
1 × 15 ml spoon/ 1 tablespoon oil	1 tablespoon oil
2 pheasants, plucked, drawn and trussed	2 pheasants, plucked, drawn and trussed
2 × 15 ml spoons/ 2 tablespoons brandy	2 tablespoons brandy
1 onion, finely chopped	1 onion, finely chopped
1 leek, thoroughly cleaned and finely chopped	1 leek, thoroughly cleaned and finely chopped
2 carrots, finely chopped	2 carrots, finely chopped
1 bay leaf	1 bay leaf
1 × 5 ml spoon/1 teaspoon chopped fresh thyme	1 teaspoon chopped fresh thyme
300 ml/½ pint single cream	1¼ cups single cream
salt	salt
freshly ground black pepper	freshly ground black pepper

Put the butter and oil in a flameproof casserole and heat gently until the butter has melted. Add the pheasants and cook until they are browned on all sides. Warm the brandy, pour over the pheasants and set alight. When the flames have died down, add the onion, leek, carrots, bay leaf and thyme. Cover and cook over a low heat for 1 hour or until the pheasants are tender. Remove the bay leaf, stir in the cream, mix well and heat through. Adjust the seasoning.

To freeze: cool quickly, cut the pheasants into serving pieces and place in a rigid container. Pour over the sauce, cover, label and freeze.

Storage life: up to 2 months

To thaw and serve: leave, covered, overnight in the refrigerator or for 4 to 5 hours at room temperature. Turn into a heavy saucepan and reheat over a gentle heat, stirring occasionally.

Serves 4

Rabbit Stew

METRIC/IMPERIAL	AMERICAN
1 rabbit, cut into serving pieces	1 rabbit, cut into serving pieces
1 × 15 ml spoon/ 1 tablespoon malt vinegar	1 tablespoon malt vinegar
40 g/1½ oz seasoned flour	⅓ cup seasoned flour
50 g/2 oz butter	¼ cup butter
1 onion, chopped	1 onion, chopped
2 carrots, sliced	2 carrots, sliced
100 g/4 oz small button mushrooms	1 cup small button mushrooms
2 × 15 ml spoons/ 2 tablespoons cornflour	2 tablespoons cornstarch
350 ml/12 fl oz chicken stock	1½ cups chicken stock
120 ml/4 fl oz dry white wine or dry cider	½ cup dry white wine or hard cider
1 × 15 ml spoon/ 1 tablespoon tomato purée	1 tablespoon tomato paste
1 × 5 ml spoon/ 1 teaspoon dried mixed herbs	½ teaspoon dried thyme
	½ teaspoon dried rosemary
2 bay leaves	2 bay leaves
salt	salt
freshly ground black pepper	freshly ground black pepper

Put the rabbit pieces into a large bowl and just cover with water. Pour over the vinegar and marinate overnight at room temperature. Drain, then dry the rabbit pieces on paper towels. Coat the pieces in the flour. Melt the butter in a saucepan and add the rabbit pieces. Fry until browned all over, then transfer to a plate.

Add the onion, carrots and mushrooms to the pan and fry gently until they are soft. Stir in the cornflour (cornstarch) to make a smooth paste. Cook for 1 minute. Stir in the stock and wine or cider and bring to the boil, stirring continuously. Stir in the tomato purée (paste), herbs and salt and pepper to taste. Return the rabbit pieces to the pan and baste well. Cover and simmer for 1¼ hours, or until the rabbit is cooked.

To freeze: cool quickly and turn into a rigid foil container. Cover, label and freeze.

Storage life: up to 2 months

To thaw and serve: thaw, covered, overnight in the refrigerator. Put, covered, into a preheated moderately hot oven (190°C/375°F, Gas Mark 5) for 1 hour.

Serves 4 to 6

*Osso buco

METRIC/IMPERIAL	AMERICAN
1.5 kg/3 lb veal knuckle or shank, sawn into 7.5 cm/ 3 inch pieces	3 lb veal knuckle or shank, sawn into 3 inch pieces
50 g/2 oz seasoned flour	½ cup seasoned flour
4 × 15 ml spoons/ 4 tablespoons olive oil	¼ cup olive oil
2 small onions, chopped	2 small onions, chopped
2 garlic cloves, crushed	2 garlic cloves, crushed
2 carrots, diced	2 carrots, diced
2 celery sticks, chopped	2 celery stalks, chopped
150 ml/¼ pint chicken stock	⅔ cup chicken stock
150 ml/¼ pint dry white wine	⅔ cup dry white wine
0.5 kg/1 lb tomatoes, blanched, peeled, deseeded and chopped	1 lb tomatoes, blanched, peeled, deseeded and chopped
1 × 5 ml spoon/1 teaspoon dried basil	1 teaspoon dried basil
1 × 5 ml spoon/1 teaspoon grated lemon rind	1 teaspoon grated lemon rind
50 g/2 oz black olives	2 oz black olives
salt	salt
freshly ground black pepper	freshly ground black pepper
chopped parsley to garnish	chopped parsley to garnish

Coat the veal pieces in the flour. Heat the oil in a flameproof casserole and add the onions, garlic, carrots and celery. Fry gently until they are soft. Add the veal pieces and fry until they are browned all over. Stir in all the remaining ingredients, except the parsley, and bring to the boil, stirring continuously. Cover and put into a preheated moderate oven (180°C/350°F, Gas Mark 4). Cook for 2 to 2½ hours, or until the meat is cooked.

To freeze: cool quickly and turn into a rigid container. Cover, label and freeze.

Storage life: up to 2 months

To thaw and serve: turn into a casserole and put into a preheated moderately hot oven (200°C/400°F, Gas Mark 6) for 1 hour. Serve garnished with chopped parsley.

Serves 4 to 6

Osso buco

Italian meatballs

METRIC/IMPERIAL	AMERICAN
0.75 kg/1½ lb lean minced beef	1½ lb lean ground beef
1 large onion, finely chopped	1 large onion, finely chopped
1 garlic clove, crushed	1 garlic clove, crushed
4 × 15 ml spoons/ 4 tablespoons dried breadcrumbs	4 tablespoons dried breadcrumbs
1 egg, beaten	1 egg, beaten
1 × 5 ml spoon/ 1 teaspoon dried marjoram	1 teaspoon dried marjoram
1 × 5 ml spoon/ 1 teaspoon dried oregano	1 teaspoon dried oregano
salt	salt
freshly ground black pepper	freshly ground black pepper
4 × 15 ml spoons/ 4 tablespoons flour	4 tablespoons flour
oil for shallow frying	oil for shallow frying
1 × 400 g/14 oz can tomatoes, puréed	1 × 14 oz can tomatoes, puréed
150 ml/¼ pint beef stock	⅔ cup beef stock
1 × 15 ml spoon/ 1 tablespoon wine vinegar	1 tablespoon wine vinegar
pinch of sugar	pinch of sugar
grated Parmesan cheese to garnish	grated Parmesan cheese to garnish

Mix together the beef, half the onion, the garlic and breadcrumbs. Combine with the beaten egg. Add half the marjoram and oregano, and salt and pepper to taste. Mix well.

Roll the mixture into about 30 balls with floured hands, then coat in the flour, seasoned with salt and pepper.

Heat 2 × 15 ml spoons/2 tablespoons of oil in a flameproof casserole. Brown the meatballs in the oil, in batches, adding more oil when necessary. Drain the meatballs on paper towels.

Fry the remaining onion in the casserole until golden. Add the tomatoes, stock, remaining herbs, vinegar and sugar. Season to taste and bring to the boil stirring. Lower the heat and return the meatballs to the casserole. Cover and transfer to a preheated moderate oven (160°C/325°F, Gas Mark 3) for 45 minutes.

To freeze: cool quickly and turn into a foil container. Cover, label and freeze.

Storage life: up to 2 months

To thaw and serve: put, covered, into a preheated moderately hot oven (200°C/400°F, Gas Mark 6) for 1 hour or until the meatballs are heated through. Serve with spaghetti, sprinkled with Parmesan cheese.

Serves 4

*Shepherd's pie

METRIC/IMPERIAL	AMERICAN
2 × 15 ml spoons/ 2 tablespoons cooking oil	2 tablespoons cooking oil
2 small onions, chopped	2 small onions, chopped
2 carrots, chopped	2 carrots, chopped
1 × 15 ml spoon/ 1 tablespoon flour	1 tablespoon flour
300 ml/½ pint beef stock	1¼ cups beef stock
2 × 15 ml spoons/ 2 tablespoons tomato ketchup	2 tablespoons tomato catsup
1 × 5 ml spoon/1 teaspoon Worcestershire sauce	1 teaspoon Worcestershire sauce
1 × 5 ml spoon/1 teaspoon dried thyme	1 teaspoon dried thyme
salt	salt
freshly ground black pepper	freshly ground black pepper
0.5 kg/1 lb cooked lamb, minced	1 lb cooked lamb, ground
0.75 kg/1½ lb potatoes, cooked and mashed	1½ lb potatoes, cooked and mashed
25 g/1 oz butter, softened	2 tablespoons butter, softened
3 × 15 ml spoons/ 3 tablespoons double cream	3 tablespoons heavy cream
1 egg, lightly beaten	1 egg, lightly beaten

Heat the oil in a saucepan and add the onions and carrots. Fry gently until they are soft. Stir in the flour to make a smooth paste, then cook for 1 minute. Stir in the stock, tomato ketchup (catsup), Worcestershire sauce, thyme, and salt and pepper to taste, and bring to the boil. Simmer for 2 to 3 minutes. Stir in the lamb and simmer until it is heated through. Turn into a rigid foil container.

Blend the mashed potatoes, butter and cream together. Spoon the mixture over the meat, to cover it completely.

To freeze: cool quickly, cover, label and freeze.

Storage life: up to 1 month

To thaw and serve: thaw, uncovered, for 4 to 5 hours at room temperature. Brush the top with beaten egg and put into a preheated hot oven (220°C/425°F, Gas Mark 7) for 20 to 30 minutes, or until the potatoes are lightly browned.

Serves 4

Pizza

*Pizza

METRIC/IMPERIAL
*100 g/4 oz risen basic
   white dough (see page
   112)*
Filling:
*15 g/½ oz butter
1 small onion, chopped
1 × 225 g/8 oz can
   tomatoes
salt
freshly ground black
   pepper
1 × 5 ml spoon/1 teaspoon
   dried oregano
50 g/2 oz Gruyère cheese,
   sliced
6 anchovy fillets, halved
8 black olives
1 × 5 ml spoon/1 teaspoon
   olive oil*

AMERICAN
*1 cup risen basic
   white dough (see page
   112)*
Filling:
*1 tablespoon butter
1 small onion, chopped
1 × ½ lb can tomatoes
salt
freshly ground black
   pepper
1 teaspoon dried oregano
2 oz Swiss cheese, sliced
6 anchovy fillets, halved
8 black olives
1 teaspoon olive oil*

Roll out the bread dough on a lightly floured surface, to a round about 20 cm/8 inches in diameter. Transfer to a well-greased baking sheet.

Melt the butter in a saucepan and add the onion. Fry gently until soft. Stir in the tomatoes and salt and pepper to taste and bring to the boil. Simmer for 15 minutes, or until the mixture is very thick.

Spoon the tomato mixture over the dough, then sprinkle over the oregano. Arrange the cheese slices on top, then the anchovies in a lattice pattern, putting an olive between each lattice. Set aside in a warm place until the dough has risen. Dribble over the oil and put the sheet into a preheated hot oven (230°C/ 450°F, Gas Mark 8). Bake for 15 to 20 minutes.

To freeze: cool quickly, wrap in heavy-duty foil, then put in a polythene (plastic) bag. Seal, label and freeze.

Storage life: up to 4 months

To thaw and serve: unwrap and transfer to a baking sheet. Put into a preheated moderately hot oven (200°C/400°F, Gas Mark 6) for 20 minutes.
Serves 2

Note: You can also prepare the pizza up to covering the top with the tomato mixture, then open freeze, wrap in heavy-duty foil, seal, label and return to the freezer. To thaw and serve it, remove the foil, then arrange the cheese, anchovies, olives and oil over the top. Put into a preheated hot oven (230°C/450°F, Gas Mark 8) for 30 to 35 minutes.

Stuffed lamb

Stuffed lamb

METRIC/IMPERIAL	AMERICAN
1.5 kg/3 lb shoulder of lamb	3 lb shoulder of lamb
2 rosemary sprigs	2 rosemary sprigs
25 g/1 oz butter	2 tablespoons butter
2 × 5 ml spoons/ 2 teaspoons flour	2 teaspoons flour
0.5 × 15 ml spoon/ ½ tablespoon tomato purée	½ tablespoon tomato paste
300 ml/½ pint chicken stock	1¼ cups chicken stock
salt	salt
freshly ground black pepper	freshly ground black pepper
Stuffing:	**Stuffing:**
90 g/3½ oz long-grain rice	½ cup long-grain rice
25 g/1 oz butter	2 tablespoons butter
100 g/4 oz lambs' liver, finely chopped	¼ lb lamb liver, finely chopped
2 small onions, finely chopped	2 small onions, finely chopped
1 garlic clove, crushed	1 garlic clove, crushed
50 g/2 oz sultanas	⅓ cup seedless white raisins
1 × 15 ml spoon/ 1 tablespoon chopped parsley	1 tablespoon chopped parsley
salt	salt
freshly ground black pepper	freshly ground black pepper

To make the stuffing, cook the rice in boiling salted water. Drain, rinse and transfer to a mixing bowl. Melt the butter in a frying pan (skillet) and add the liver. Fry gently until it loses its pinkness. Add the onions and garlic and fry until they are soft. Transfer to the rice, then stir in the sultanas (raisins), parsley and salt and pepper to taste.

To freeze: put the meat into a polythene (plastic) bag, seal, label and freeze. Put the stuffing into a separate polythene (plastic) bag, seal, label and freeze.

Storage life: up to 2 months

To thaw and serve: thaw both meat and stuffing overnight in the refrigerator. Stuff the stuffing mixture into the meat, then secure with skewers or trussing thread. Put into a roasting pan with the rosemary and dot with the butter. Put the pan into a preheated moderate oven (180°C/350°F, Gas Mark 4) for 1¾ to 2 hours, or until the lamb is cooked. Transfer the meat to a serving dish.

Pour off all but 1 × 15 ml spoon/1 tablespoon of the cooking liquid from the pan. Stir in the flour to make a smooth paste. Cook for 1 minute. Stir in the tomato purée (paste), stock and salt and pepper to taste and bring to the boil. Simmer for 2 to 3 minutes, stirring continuously. Pour into a sauce boat and serve with the meat.

Serves 6 to 8

Coq au vin

METRIC/IMPERIAL	AMERICAN
1.75 kg/4 lb roasting chicken, jointed	4 lb roasting chicken, jointed
50 g/2 oz flour	½ cup flour
salt	salt
freshly ground black pepper	freshly ground black pepper
50 g/2 oz butter	¼ cup butter
2 × 15 ml spoons/ 2 tablespoons oil	2 tablespoons oil
100 g/4 oz streaky bacon, chopped	¼ lb fatty bacon, chopped
225 g/8 oz button onions, peeled	½ lb baby onions, peeled
2 garlic cloves, chopped	2 garlic cloves, chopped
1 × 15 ml spoon/ 1 tablespoon tomato purée	1 tablespoon tomato paste
pinch of sugar	pinch of sugar
2 × 15 ml spoons/ 2 tablespoons brandy	2 tablespoons brandy
300 ml/½ pint red wine	1¼ cups red wine
150 ml/¼ pint beef stock	⅔ cup beef stock
1 bouquet garni	1 bouquet garni
225 g/8 oz button mushrooms	2 cups button mushrooms

Coat the chicken pieces in the flour, well seasoned with salt and pepper. Put the butter and oil in a flameproof casserole and heat gently until the butter has melted. Quickly brown the chicken pieces on all sides, then remove from the casserole. Add the bacon, onions and garlic and cook gently until golden brown. Sprinkle in any remaining flour, the tomato purée (paste) and the sugar, and stir well. Return the chicken pieces to the casserole. Warm the brandy, pour over the chicken and set alight. Allow to flame for 1 minute, then pour in the wine and stock. Add the bouquet garni, cover and simmer over a low heat for 30 to 40 minutes or until the chicken is cooked. Add the mushrooms and simmer for another 15 minutes.

To freeze: cool quickly and turn into a rigid container. Cover, label and freeze.

Storage life: up to 2 months

To thaw and serve: thaw, covered, overnight in the refrigerator. Turn into a flameproof casserole and reheat gently.

Serves 4

Sweet sour spareribs

Sweet sour spareribs

METRIC/IMPERIAL
1 kg/2 lb American-style
  pork spareribs
1 × 15 ml spoon/
  1 tablespoon cooking oil
1 onion, chopped
1 carrot, cut into thin
  strips
150 ml/¼ pint pineapple
  juice
5 × 15 ml spoons/
  5 tablespoons wine
  vinegar
1 × 15 ml spoon/
  1 tablespoon
  Worcestershire sauce
1 × 5 ml spoon/1 teaspoon
  soy sauce
50 g/2 oz brown sugar
1 × 15 ml spoon/
  1 tablespoon cornflour
4 × 15 ml spoons/
  4 tablespoons water
juice and grated rind of
  ½ lemon
salt
freshly ground black
  pepper

AMERICAN
2 lb pork spareribs
1 tablespoon cooking oil
1 onion, chopped
1 carrot, cut into thin
  strips
⅔ cup pineapple juice
⅓ cup wine vinegar
1 tablespoon
  Worcestershire sauce
1 teaspoon soy sauce
⅓ cup brown sugar
1 tablespoon cornstarch
¼ cup water
juice and grated rind of
  ½ lemon
salt
freshly ground black
  pepper

Put the spareribs into a roasting pan and put the pan into a preheated hot oven (220°C/425°F, Gas Mark 7). Cook for 20 minutes. Remove the ribs, drain off the fat and replace the ribs in the pan.

Heat the oil in a saucepan and add the onion and carrot. Fry gently until they are soft. Pour over the pineapple juice, vinegar, Worcestershire sauce, soy sauce and sugar, stirring until the sugar dissolves. Simmer for 20 minutes, stirring occasionally. Mix the cornflour (cornstarch) and water together, then stir into the sauce with the lemon juice and rind and salt and pepper to taste. Bring to the boil, stirring continuously. Simmer for 2 to 3 minutes, or until the sauce thickens and becomes translucent.

Pour the sauce over the ribs. Cover and put into a preheated moderate oven (180°C/350°F, Gas Mark 4). Cook for 40 minutes, basting occasionally.
To freeze: cool quickly, wrap in heavy-duty foil and put in a polythene (plastic) bag. Seal, label and freeze.
Storage life: up to 2 months
To thaw and serve: unwrap and put into a roasting pan. Cover and put into a preheated moderately hot oven (200°C/400°F, Gas Mark 6) for 45 minutes. Remove the cover for the last 15 minutes.
Serves 4

Summer chicken stew

METRIC/IMPERIAL
5 × 15 ml spoons/
  5 tablespoons cooking oil
4 chicken pieces
1 onion, chopped
1 garlic clove, crushed
100 g/4 oz mushrooms,
  sliced
225 g/8 oz marrow, peeled,
  deseeded and cubed
8 tomatoes, blanched,
  peeled and chopped
salt
freshly ground black
  pepper
1 × 5 ml spoon/1 teaspoon
  dried basil
1 × 5 ml spoon/1 teaspoon
  grated orange rind

AMERICAN
⅓ cup cooking oil
4 chicken pieces
1 onion, chopped
1 garlic clove, crushed
1 cup sliced mushrooms
½ lb summer squash,
  peeled, deseeded and
  cubed
8 tomatoes, blanched,
  peeled and chopped
salt
freshly ground black
  pepper
1 teaspoon dried basil
1 teaspoon grated orange
  rind

Heat the oil in a saucepan and add the chicken pieces. Fry until they are browned all over. Transfer to a plate. Add the onion and garlic and fry gently until they are soft. Add all the remaining ingredients and bring to the boil. Return the chicken pieces to the pan. Cover and simmer for 45 minutes, or until the chicken is cooked.
To freeze: cool quickly and turn into a rigid container. Cover, label and freeze.
Storage life: up to 2 months
To thaw and serve: thaw overnight in the refrigerator. Turn into a saucepan and bring slowly to the boil, stirring continuously. Simmer for 10 minutes.
Serves 4

Rouladen

*Rouladen

METRIC/IMPERIAL	AMERICAN
4 slices beef topside, cut 5 mm/¼ inch thick	4 slices beef round, cut ¼ inch thick
4 × 5 ml spoons/ 4 teaspoons horseradish cream	4 teaspoons horseradish cream
salt	salt
freshly ground black pepper	freshly ground black pepper
2 small carrots, cut into strips	2 small carrots, cut into strips
1 small onion, finely chopped	1 small onion, finely chopped
1 celery stick, cut into strips	1 celery stalk, cut into strips
25 g/1 oz seasoned flour	¼ cup seasoned flour
25 g/1 oz butter	2 tablespoons butter
450 ml/¾ pint tomato juice	2 cups tomato juice
4 × 15 ml spoons/ 4 tablespoons red wine	¼ cup red wine
chopped parsley to garnish	chopped parsley to garnish

Put the meat slices between 2 sheets of dampened greaseproof (waxed) paper and pound until they are very thin. Remove the paper. Spread each slice with horseradish, and sprinkle with salt and pepper. Arrange the vegetable pieces on top, then roll up Swiss (jelly) roll style and secure with string. Coat the rolls in the flour.

Melt the butter in a frying pan (skillet) and add the rolls. Fry until they are browned all over. Pour over the tomato juice and wine, and bring to the boil. Cover and simmer for 2 hours, or until the meat is cooked.

To freeze: cool quickly, then carefully turn into a rigid container. Cover, label and freeze.

Storage life: up to 2 months

To thaw and serve: turn into a casserole and put into a preheated moderate oven (180°C/350°F, Gas Mark 4) for 45 minutes. Serve garnished with chopped parsley.

Serves 4

*Veal marengo

METRIC/IMPERIAL
50 g/2 oz butter
1 kg/2 lb lean stewing
veal, cubed
1 large onion, chopped
1 garlic clove, crushed
1 × 15 ml spoon/
1 tablespoon flour
250 ml/8 fl oz chicken
stock
250 ml/8 fl oz dry white
wine
1 × 400 g/14 oz can
tomatoes, drained and
puréed
1 × 5 ml spoon/1 teaspoon
dried thyme
1 bay leaf
salt
freshly ground black
pepper
225 g/8 oz mushrooms,
sliced

AMERICAN
¼ cup butter
2 lb lean stewing veal,
cubed
1 large onion, chopped
1 garlic clove, crushed
1 tablespoon flour
1 cup chicken stock
1 cup dry white wine
1 × 14 oz can tomatoes,
drained and puréed
1 teaspoon dried thyme
1 bay leaf
salt
freshly ground black
pepper
2 cups sliced mushrooms

Melt the butter in a saucepan and add the veal cubes. Fry until they are browned all over. Add the onion and garlic and fry gently until they are soft. Stir in the flour to make a smooth paste. Stir in the stock and wine and bring to the boil, stirring continuously. Simmer for 2 to 3 minutes. Stir in the puréed tomatoes, herbs and salt and pepper to taste. Cover and simmer for 1 hour. Add the mushrooms, re-cover and simmer for a further 30 minutes, or until the meat is cooked. Remove the bay leaf.
To freeze: cool quickly and turn into a rigid container. Cover, label and freeze.
Storage life: up to 2 months
To thaw and serve: turn into an ovenproof dish, cover and put into a preheated moderately hot oven (200°C/400°F, Gas Mark 6) for 45 minutes, stirring occasionally.
Serves 4 to 6

Steak and kidney pudding

METRIC/IMPERIAL
0.5 kg/1 lb stewing steak,
cubed
225 g/8 oz ox kidney,
trimmed and cubed
25 g/1 oz seasoned flour
4 × 15 ml spoons/
4 tablespoons cooking oil
2 onions, chopped
150 ml/¼ pint beef stock
Pastry:
225 g/8 oz self-raising
flour
1 × 2.5 ml spoon/
½ teaspoon salt
1 × 5 ml spoon/
1 teaspoon baking
powder
100 g/4 oz shredded beef
suet
150 ml/¼ pint water

AMERICAN
1 lb chuck steak, cubed
½ lb beef kidney, trimmed
and cubed
¼ cup seasoned flour
¼ cup cooking oil
2 onions, chopped
⅔ cup beef stock

Pastry:
2 cups self-rising
flour
½ teaspoon salt
1 teaspoon baking
powder
¼ lb shredded beef suet
⅔ cup water

Coat the steak and kidney in the seasoned flour. Heat the oil in a saucepan and add the onions. Fry gently until soft. Add the meat cubes and fry until they are browned all over. Stir in the stock and bring to the boil. Cover and simmer for 2 to 2½ hours, or until the meat is cooked. Set aside to cool.

To make the pastry, sift the flour, salt and baking powder into a mixing bowl. Stir in the suet and enough cold water to make a smooth, slightly soft dough. Turn out onto a lightly floured surface and knead lightly for 2 minutes, or until smooth. Roll out two-thirds of the pastry dough and use it to line a well-greased 1.2 litre/2 pint/5 cup freezerproof pudding basin (ovenproof bowl). Spoon the filling into the pastry case. Roll out the remaining pastry dough into a circle large enough to form a lid over the filling. Dampen the edges of the pudding, then cover and crimp to seal.
To freeze: wrap in heavy-duty foil, seal, label and freeze.
Storage life: up to 1 month
To thaw and serve: thaw, wrapped, overnight in the refrigerator. Cover with greased foil with a pleat in the centre to allow for expansion. Secure foil with string. Steam the pudding for 2 hours, adding more boiling water when necessary.
Serves 4

VEGETABLES

Rosti

Rosti

METRIC/IMPERIAL
1 kg/2 lb potatoes, cooked
  and cooled
75 g/3 oz Gruyère cheese,
  grated
salt
freshly ground black
  pepper
75 g/3 oz butter
100 g/4 oz streaky bacon,
  cut into strips

AMERICAN
2 lb potatoes, cooked
  and cooled
¾ cup grated Swiss cheese
salt
freshly ground black
  pepper
6 tablespoons butter
¼ lb fatty bacon, cut into
  strips

Grate the potatoes into a bowl, then stir in the grated cheese and salt and pepper to taste. Melt a third of the butter in a frying pan (skillet) and add the bacon strips. Fry until they are golden brown. Drain the strips on paper towels, then stir them into the potato mixture. Turn the mixture onto a large piece of heavy-duty foil and shape into a round.
To freeze: cover completely with heavy-duty foil, seal, label and freeze.
Storage life: up to 2 months
To thaw and serve: melt the remaining butter in a large frying pan (skillet) and add the potato cake. Thaw gently over a very low heat. Cook gently for 15 minutes on each side, or until it is golden brown.
Serves 4

Leeks mornay

METRIC/IMPERIAL
8 large leeks, thoroughly
  cleaned and trimmed
8 thin slices cooked ham
600 ml/1 pint mornay
  sauce (see page 33)
2 × 15 ml spoons/
  2 tablespoons grated
  cheese
2 × 15 ml spoons/
  2 tablespoons fresh
  breadcrumbs

AMERICAN
8 large leeks, thoroughly
  cleaned and trimmed
8 thin slices cooked ham
2½ cups mornay sauce
  (see page 33)
2 tablespoons grated
  cheese
2 tablespoons fresh
  breadcrumbs

Put the leeks into a saucepan of boiling, salted water and cook for 20 minutes, or until they are tender. Drain. Wrap a slice of ham around each leek, then transfer to a well-greased rigid foil container, seam side down. Pour over the mornay sauce, then sprinkle over the grated cheese and breadcrumbs.
To freeze: cool quickly, cover, label and freeze.
Storage life: up to 2 months
To thaw and serve: thaw for 4 to 5 hours at room temperature. Put into a preheated moderately hot oven (190°C/375°F, Gas Mark 5) for 30 to 40 minutes, or until the sauce is lightly browned.
Serves 2 to 4

Stuffed peppers

METRIC/IMPERIAL	AMERICAN
25 g/1 oz butter	2 tablespoons butter
100 g/4 oz lean bacon, chopped	¼ lb Canadian bacon, chopped
3 large tomatoes, blanched, peeled and chopped	3 large tomatoes, blanched, peeled and chopped
1 garlic clove, crushed	1 garlic clove, crushed
1 × 5 ml spoon/1 teaspoon dried mixed herbs	½ teaspoon dried marjoram ½ teaspoon dried oregano
225 g/8 oz cooked rice	3 cups cooked rice
salt	salt
freshly ground black pepper	freshly ground black pepper
4 green peppers	4 green peppers
50 g/2 oz Cheddar cheese, grated	½ cup grated Cheddar cheese

Melt the butter in a frying pan (skillet) and add the bacon. Fry until it is golden brown. Transfer the mixture to a mixing bowl, then stir in the tomatoes, garlic, herbs, rice and salt and pepper to taste.

Cut the peppers in half lengthways and remove the seeds and pith. Blanch for 3 minutes in boiling water, then drain. Arrange the pepper halves in foil containers and stuff the cavities with the rice mixture. Sprinkle over the grated cheese.

To freeze: cool quickly, cover, label and freeze.

Storage life: up to 2 months

To thaw and serve: put, covered, into a preheated hot oven (220°C/425°F, Gas Mark 7) for 1 hour. Uncover and cook for a further 20 minutes, to brown.

Serves 4

*Carrots and turnips in onion sauce

METRIC/IMPERIAL	AMERICAN
4 large carrots, chopped	4 large carrots, chopped
1 small turnip, chopped	1 small turnip, chopped
Sauce:	**Sauce:**
25 g/1 oz butter	2 tablespoons butter
1 large onion, chopped	1 large onion, chopped
25 g/1 oz flour	¼ cup flour
300 ml/½ pint milk	1¼ cups milk
salt	salt
freshly ground black pepper	freshly ground black pepper

Blanch the carrots and turnip in boiling water for 3 minutes, then drain and set aside.

To make the sauce, melt the butter in a saucepan and add the onion. Fry gently until soft. Stir in the flour to make a smooth paste. Cook for 1 minute. Stir in the milk, and bring to the boil. Simmer for 2 to 3 minutes, stirring continuously. Stir in the vegetables and salt and pepper to taste, and simmer for a further 2 minutes.

To freeze: cool quickly and turn into a rigid container. Cover, label and freeze.

Storage life: up to 3 months

To thaw and serve: turn into a saucepan with 1 × 15 ml spoon/1 tablespoon of water and thaw over a very low heat. Bring the mixture to the boil, stirring occasionally.

Serves 4

*Braised red cabbage

METRIC/IMPERIAL	AMERICAN
1 medium red cabbage, shredded	1 medium red cabbage, shredded
0.5 kg/1 lb cooking apples, peeled, cored and chopped	1 lb baking apples, peeled, cored and chopped
150 ml/¼ pint water	⅔ cup water
3 × 15 ml spoons/ 3 tablespoons sugar	3 tablespoons sugar
1 × 5 ml spoon/1 teaspoon salt	1 teaspoon salt
5 cloves	5 cloves
4 × 15 ml spoons/ 4 tablespoons vinegar	¼ cup vinegar
50 g/2 oz butter	¼ cup butter

Put the cabbage, apples, water, sugar, salt and cloves into a flameproof casserole and bring to the boil. Stir in the remaining ingredients, cover, and put the casserole into a preheated moderate oven (160°C/325°F, Gas Mark 3). Braise for 2 hours.

To freeze: cool quickly and turn into a rigid container. Cover, label and freeze.

Storage life: up to 4 months

To thaw and serve: thaw for 5 to 6 hours at room temperature. Turn into a casserole and put into a preheated moderate oven (160°C/325°F, Gas Mark 3) for 30 minutes, stirring occasionally.

Serves 4 to 6

Braised red cabbage

French fries

METRIC/IMPERIAL
1 kg/2 lb potatoes, cut into strips
oil for deep frying

AMERICAN
2 lb potatoes, cut into strips
oil for deep frying

Blanch the French fries in boiling water for 2 minutes, then drain. Pat dry with paper towels. Deep fry in hot oil in batches, for about 5 minutes, or until they are golden brown. Drain on paper towels.

To freeze: cool quickly, then open freeze. When frozen, turn into polythene (plastic) bags, seal, label and return to the freezer.

Storage life: up to 3 weeks

To thaw and serve: arrange the frozen French fries on a baking sheet and put into a preheated moderately hot oven (200°C/400°F, Gas Mark 6) for 20 minutes.

Serves 6

French fries

Cauliflower cheese

METRIC/IMPERIAL
1 medium cauliflower, broken into florets
40 g/1½ oz butter
40 g/1½ oz flour
450 ml/¾ pint milk
75 g/3 oz Cheddar cheese, grated
1 × 2.5 ml spoon/ ½ teaspoon dry mustard
salt
freshly ground black pepper
1 × 15 ml spoon/ 1 tablespoon grated Parmesan cheese
2 × 15 ml spoons/ 2 tablespoons dry breadcrumbs

AMERICAN
1 medium cauliflower, broken into florets
3 tablespoons butter
⅓ cup flour
2 cups milk
¾ cup grated Cheddar cheese
½ teaspoon dry mustard
salt
freshly ground black pepper
1 tablespoon grated Parmesan cheese
2 tablespoons dry breadcrumbs

Cook the cauliflower in boiling water until it is barely cooked. Drain, reserving about 4 × 15 ml spoons/ 4 tablespoons/¼ cup of the cooking liquid. Transfer to a rigid foil container.

Melt the butter in a saucepan and stir in the flour to make a smooth paste. Cook for 1 minute. Stir in the milk and bring to the boil, stirring continuously. Stir in the grated Cheddar cheese, mustard, reserved cooking liquid and salt and pepper to taste. Continue stirring until the cheese has melted. Pour over the cauliflower and sprinkle on the grated Parmesan cheese and breadcrumbs.

To freeze: cover, label and freeze.

Storage life: up to 2 months

To thaw and serve: put, uncovered, into a preheated moderately hot oven (200°C/400°F, Gas Mark 6) for 30 minutes.

Serves 4

*Courgettes (zucchini) Italian style

METRIC/IMPERIAL
4 × 15 ml spoons/ 4 tablespoons cooking oil
6 courgettes, thinly sliced
1 large onion, chopped
2 garlic cloves, crushed
1 × 5 ml spoon/1 teaspoon dried basil
pinch of paprika
4 tomatoes, blanched, peeled and chopped
2 × 15 ml spoons/ 2 tablespoons tomato purée
1 bay leaf
salt
freshly ground black pepper

AMERICAN
¼ cup cooking oil
6 zucchini, thinly sliced
1 large onion, chopped
2 garlic cloves, crushed
1 teaspoon dried basil
pinch of paprika
4 tomatoes, blanched, peeled and chopped
2 tablespoons tomato paste
1 bay leaf
salt
freshly ground black pepper

Heat the oil in a large saucepan and add the courgettes (zucchini), onion and garlic. Fry gently until the onion is soft. Stir in all the remaining ingredients and bring to the boil, stirring continuously. Cover and simmer for 20 minutes, or until the courgettes (zucchini) are cooked.

To freeze: cool quickly and turn into a rigid container. Cover, label and freeze.

Storage life: up to 4 months

To thaw and serve: to eat cold, thaw, uncovered, for 5 to 6 hours at room temperature. To eat hot, turn into a saucepan and thaw over a very low heat. Simmer for 30 minutes, stirring occasionally.

Serves 4

*Harvard beets

METRIC/IMPERIAL	AMERICAN
50 g/2 oz brown sugar	⅓ cup brown sugar
1 × 15 ml spoon/ 1 tablespoon flour	1 tablespoon flour
120 ml/4 fl oz wine vinegar	½ cup wine vinegar
2 × 15 ml spoons/ 2 tablespoons water	2 tablespoons water
0.5 kg/1 lb cooked beetroots, skinned and sliced	1 lb cooked beets, skinned and sliced
salt	salt
freshly ground black pepper	freshly ground black pepper

Put the sugar and flour into a saucepan and slowly stir in the vinegar and water. Bring to the boil, stirring continuously. Simmer for 2 to 3 minutes. Stir in the beetroots (beets) and salt and pepper to taste and simmer for a further 10 minutes.
To freeze: cool quickly and turn into a rigid container. Cover, label and freeze.
Storage life: up to 6 months
To thaw and serve: turn into a saucepan and add 2 × 15 ml spoons/2 tablespoons of water. Thaw over a very low heat. Cook for 30 minutes, stirring occasionally.
Serves 4

Harvard beets

Potato croquettes

METRIC/IMPERIAL	AMERICAN
1 kg/2 lb potatoes, cooked	2 lb potatoes, cooked
50 g/2 oz butter, softened	¼ cup butter, softened
1 egg, beaten	1 egg, beaten
1 × 15 ml spoon/ 1 tablespoon cream	1 tablespoon cream
1 × 2.5 ml spoon/ ½ teaspoon dry mustard	½ teaspoon dry mustard
salt	salt
freshly ground black pepper	freshly ground black pepper
50 g/2 oz seasoned flour	½ cup seasoned flour
2 eggs, beaten	2 eggs, beaten
50 g/2 oz fresh breadcrumbs	1 cup fresh breadcrumbs
oil for deep frying	oil for deep frying

Put the potatoes into a bowl and mash until smooth. Beat in the butter, egg, cream, mustard and salt and pepper until they are blended. Chill in the refrigerator until the mixture is firm and cold.

Divide the mixture into about 16 portions, then shape each portion into a fat sausage shape by rolling between your hands. Dip the croquettes, one by one, into the seasoned flour, then the egg and finally the breadcrumbs, making sure they are all thoroughly coated. Chill for 30 minutes.

Deep fry the croquettes, a few at a time, in hot oil for 4 to 5 minutes, or until they are crisp and golden brown. Drain on paper towels.
To freeze: cool quickly, then open freeze. When frozen, turn into a polythene (plastic) bag, seal, label and return to the freezer.
Storage life: up to 3 months
To thaw and serve: arrange the frozen croquettes on a baking sheet and put into a preheated moderately hot oven (200°C/400°F, Gas Mark 6) for 20 minutes.
Serves 8

DESSERTS

Apple flan

Apple flan

METRIC/IMPERIAL
*175 g/6 oz frozen
  shortcrust pastry, thawed
450 ml/¾ pint apple purée
50 g/2 oz sugar
grated rind of 1 lemon
2 large cooking apples,
  peeled, cored and thinly
  sliced
1 × 15 ml spoon/
  1 tablespoon sieved
  apricot jam
2 × 5 ml spoons/
  2 teaspoons water
1 × 5 ml spoon/1 teaspoon
  lemon juice*

AMERICAN
*6 oz frozen basic pie
  dough, thawed
2 cups applesauce
¼ cup sugar
grated rind of 1 lemon
2 large baking apples,
  peeled, cored and thinly
  sliced
1 tablespoon strained
  apricot jam
2 teaspoons water
1 teaspoon lemon juice*

Roll out the pastry dough on a lightly floured surface and use to line a well-greased 20 cm/8 inch flan dish (pie pan). Put the dish on a baking sheet. Beat the apple purée (applesauce), sugar and lemon rind together, then spoon into the pastry case (pie shell). Arrange the apple slices attractively over the surface.

Put the sheet into a preheated moderately hot oven (200°C/400°F, Gas Mark 6) and bake for 25 to 30 minutes, or until the pastry is golden brown. Set aside to cool.

Put the jam, water and lemon juice into a saucepan and heat until syrupy. Brush the mixture over the filling.

To freeze: cool quickly, then open freeze. When frozen, wrap in heavy-duty foil, put in a polythene (plastic) bag, seal, label and return to the freezer.

Storage life: up to 6 months

To thaw and serve: put, covered, into a preheated moderately hot oven (200°C/400°F, Gas Mark 6) for 5 minutes. Uncover and bake for a further 25 minutes.

Serves 4 to 6

Apricot cake

METRIC/IMPERIAL
3 eggs, separated
100 g/4 oz caster sugar
1 × 2.5 ml spoon/
½ teaspoon ground
allspice
50 g/2 oz semolina
25 g/1 oz ground almonds
150 ml/¼ pint double
cream, stiffly beaten
1 × 400 g/14 oz can
apricot pie filling

AMERICAN
3 eggs, separated
½ cup superfine sugar
½ teaspoon ground allspice
⅓ cup semolina flour
¼ cup ground almonds
⅔ cup heavy cream,
stiffly beaten
1 × 14 oz can apricot pie
filling

Line a greased 20 cm/8 inch sandwich tin (layer cake pan) with greaseproof (waxed) paper. Put the egg yolks and sugar into a heatproof bowl and set over a pan of simmering water. Heat over a low heat, beating continuously until the mixture is pale and thick. Remove the bowl from the pan and continue beating until the mixture cools. Gently fold in the allspice, semolina and almonds. Beat the egg whites until they form stiff peaks, then fold into the egg yolk mixture. Pour into the prepared tin (pan).

Put the tin (pan) into a preheated moderate oven (180°C/350°F, Gas Mark 4) and bake for 25 to 30 minutes, or until the cake springs back when lightly pressed with a fingertip. Turn out onto a wire rack, remove the paper and set aside to cool.
To freeze: when cold, wrap in heavy-duty foil, or put in a polythene (plastic) bag. Seal, label and freeze.
Storage life: up to 4 months
To thaw and serve: thaw, uncovered, for 2 hours at room temperature. Split in half. Combine the cream and pie filling and spread generously over the bottom half. Cover with the top half and serve.
Serves 6

Apple and orange dessert

METRIC/IMPERIAL
300 ml/½ pint apple purée
2 × 15 ml spoons/
2 tablespoons brown sugar
1.5 × 5 ml spoons/
1½ teaspoons grated
orange rind
2 eggs, separated
150 ml/¼ pint double
cream, stiffly beaten

AMERICAN
1¼ cups applesauce
2 tablespoons brown sugar
1½ teaspoons grated
orange rind
2 eggs, separated
⅔ cup heavy cream,
stiffly beaten

Put the apple purée (applesauce), sugar and orange rind into a heatproof bowl and set over a saucepan of simmering water. Gently beat in the egg yolks and heat over a low heat, stirring continuously, until the mixture is thick and smooth. Remove the bowl from the pan and set aside to cool.

Beat the egg whites until they form stiff peaks, then quickly fold into the apple purée (applesauce) with the cream.
To freeze: turn into a freezerproof serving dish, cover and freeze. When frozen, dip the bottom of the dish into boiling water for 2 seconds, then invert the dessert on to a plate. Put in a polythene (plastic) bag, seal, label and return to the freezer.
Storage life: up to 3 months
To thaw and serve: return to the serving dish and thaw for 6 hours in the refrigerator.
Serves 4

*Blackcurrant mousse

METRIC/IMPERIAL
1 packet blackcurrant
jelly
0.5 kg/1 lb blackcurrants
3 × 15 ml spoons/
3 tablespoons water
75 g/3 oz sugar
3 eggs, separated

AMERICAN
1 package blackcurrant-
flavored powdered
gelatin
1 lb blackcurrants
3 tablespoons water
⅓ cup sugar
3 eggs, separated

Dissolve the jelly (gelatin) in 150 ml/¼ pint/⅔ cup of boiling water. Stir in up to 300 ml/½ pint/1¼ cups of cold water and set aside until the jelly (gelatin) has thickened and is almost set.

Put the blackcurrants, water and sugar into a saucepan over a gentle heat and stir continuously until the sugar has dissolved. Cover and simmer until the blackcurrants are tender. Pour the mixture through a sieve (strainer) into the jelly (gelatin) and stir to mix. Beat the egg yolks into the mixture. Beat the egg whites until they form stiff peaks, then fold into the jelly (gelatin) mixture. Turn into a rigid container.
To freeze: cover, label and freeze.
Storage life: up to 3 months
To thaw and serve: thaw for 6 hours in the refrigerator.
Serves 6

*Baked Alaska

METRIC/IMPERIAL	AMERICAN
100 g/4 oz trifle sponges, halved	1 stale sponge cake, broken into large pieces
4 × 15 ml spoons/ 4 tablespoons sherry	¼ cup sherry
3 egg whites	3 egg whites
175 g/6 oz caster sugar	¾ cup superfine sugar
600 ml/1 pint vanilla ice cream	2½ cups vanilla ice cream

Use the trifle sponges (sponge pieces) to line a freezer-proof dish. Sprinkle over the sherry and set aside to soak for 10 minutes. Beat the egg whites until they form stiff peaks, then beat in half the sugar and beat for a further 1 minute. Fold in the remaining sugar. Put the ice cream over the trifle sponges (sponge pieces), leaving 1 cm/½ inch around the edges. Spread the meringue mixture over the ice cream and sponges to cover them completely.

To freeze: open freeze immediately. When frozen, wrap lightly in heavy-duty foil, seal and return to the freezer. (The meringue will remain slightly soft.)

Storage life: up to 3 months

To thaw and serve: unwrap and put immediately into a preheated hot oven (220°C/425°F, Gas Mark 7) for 5 minutes, or until crisp and brown. Serve at once.

Serves 6

Baked Alaska

*Chocolate mousse

METRIC/IMPERIAL	AMERICAN
175 g/6 oz plain chocolate, broken into pieces	6 squares semi-sweet cooking chocolate, broken into pieces
3 × 15 ml spoons/ 3 tablespoons rum	3 tablespoons rum
2 × 15 ml spoons/ 2 tablespoons water	2 tablespoons water
2 eggs, separated	2 eggs, separated
few drops vanilla essence	few drops vanilla extract
75 g/3 oz caster sugar	⅓ cup superfine sugar
300 ml/½ pint double cream	1¼ cups heavy cream
150 ml/¼ pint single cream	⅔ cup light cream

Line the base of a 20 cm/8 inch cake tin (pan) or soufflé dish with greaseproof (waxed) paper. Put the chocolate, rum and water into a heatproof bowl and set over a pan of simmering water. Heat over a low heat, stirring continuously, until the chocolate has melted and the mixture is thick and smooth. Remove the bowl from the pan and beat in the egg yolks and vanilla. Set aside to cool.

Beat the egg whites until they form stiff peaks, then gradually beat in the sugar. Quickly fold the chocolate mixture into the egg whites until thoroughly blended. Beat the double (heavy) and single (light) creams together until they form stiff peaks. Fold into the chocolate mixture. Pour into the cake tin (pan) or dish.

To freeze: freeze the mousse until firm, then dip the tin (pan) or dish into boiling water for 2 seconds. Invert the mousse into a polythene (plastic) bag, seal, label and return to the freezer.

Storage life: up to 3 months

To thaw and serve: turn out onto a serving dish and thaw for 5 to 10 minutes at room temperature.

Serves 4

*Baked apples

METRIC/IMPERIAL	AMERICAN
4 large cooking apples	4 large baking apples
1 × 5 ml spoon/1 teaspoon ground allspice	1 teaspoon ground allspice
1 × 15 ml spoon/ 1 tablespoon mincemeat	1 tablespoon mincemeat
2 × 15 ml spoons/ 2 tablespoons sultanas	2 tablespoons seedless white raisins
120 ml/4 fl oz dry cider	½ cup hard cider or unsweetened apple juice
75 g/3 oz soft brown sugar	½ cup soft brown sugar
25 g/1 oz butter, cut into into small pieces	2 tablespoons butter, cut into small pieces

Hollow out the centres of the apples and core them. Make a shallow cut around the skin. Transfer the apples to a baking dish (pan). Mix the allspice, mincemeat and sultanas (raisins) together. Spoon equal quantities into the apple cavities. Pour over the cider and scatter the sugar and the butter pieces over the apples.

Put the dish (pan) into preheated moderate oven (180°C/350°F, Gas Mark 4) and bake for 1 hour, or until the apples are cooked through, basting occasionally with the cooking liquid.

To freeze: cool quickly and turn the apples and cooking liquid into a rigid container. Cover, label and freeze.

Storage life: up to 9 months

To thaw and serve: thaw, covered, for 5 to 6 hours in the refrigerator. Or thaw and put into a preheated moderate oven (180°C/350°F, Gas Mark 4) for 20 minutes.

Serves 4

Baked Apple

*Bombe regina

METRIC/IMPERIAL	AMERICAN
300 ml/½ pint double cream	1¼ cups heavy cream
2 × 15 ml spoons/ 2 tablespoons brandy	2 tablespoons brandy
1 × 15 ml spoon/ 1 tablespoon sugar	1 tablespoon sugar
100 g/4 oz meringue, roughly chopped	¼ lb meringue, roughly chopped

Beat the cream until it forms stiff peaks. Beat in the brandy and sugar, then fold in the meringue pieces. Pour the mixture into a lightly oiled 600 ml/1 pint/ 2½ cup freezerproof mould or foil-lined pudding basin (bowl).

To freeze: cover, label and freeze.

Storage life: up to 3 months

To thaw and serve: unwrap and remove from the mould. Thaw for 15 minutes in the refrigerator.

Serves 4

Butterscotch sauce

METRIC/IMPERIAL	AMERICAN
1 × 15 ml spoon/ 1 tablespoon golden syrup	1 tablespoon light corn syrup
1 × 15 ml spoon/ 1 tablespoon lemon juice	1 tablespoon lemon juice
1 × 15 ml spoon/ 1 tablespoon brown sugar	1 tablespoon brown sugar
15 g/½ oz butter	1 tablespoon butter
1.5 × 5 ml spoons/ 1½ teaspoons custard powder	1½ teaspoons custard powder
150 ml/¼ pint water	⅔ cup water

Put the syrup, lemon juice, sugar and butter into a saucepan and simmer until the butter has melted, stirring continuously. Mix the custard powder and water to a smooth paste and stir into the syrup mixture. Bring to the boil, stirring continuously, then simmer for 2 to 3 minutes, or until the sauce has thickened slightly.

To freeze: cool quickly and turn into a rigid container. Cover, label and freeze.

Storage life: up to 3 months

To thaw and serve: turn into a saucepan and thaw over a very low heat. Heat until hot but not boiling.

Serves 4

Christmas pudding

Christmas pudding

METRIC/IMPERIAL
175 g/6 oz self-raising
  flour
1 × 5 ml spoon/1 teaspoon
  ground allspice
1 × 2.5 ml spoon/
  ½ teaspoon grated nutmeg
1 × 5 ml spoon/1 teaspoon
  salt
0.5 kg/1 lb fresh
  breadcrumbs
0.5 kg/1 lb shredded suet
100 g/4 oz chopped
  candied peel
100 g/4 oz chopped,
  blanched almonds
grated rind of 2 oranges
1.5 kg/3 lb chopped
  sultanas
225 g/8 oz currants
350 g/12 oz brown sugar
4 × 15 ml spoons/
  4 tablespoons treacle
6 eggs
600 ml/1 pint stout

AMERICAN
1½ cups self-rising flour
1 teaspoon ground
  allspice
½ teaspoon grated nutmeg
1 teaspoon salt
8 cups fresh
  breadcrumbs
1 lb shredded suet
⅔ cup chopped candied
  peel
1 cup chopped, blanched
  almonds
grated rind of 2 oranges
8 cups seedless white
  raisins
1⅓ cups currants
2 cups brown sugar
4 tablespoons molasses
6 eggs
2½ cups stout or beer

Sift the flour, spices and salt into a large bowl. Stir in the breadcrumbs, suet, candied peel, almonds, orange rind, dried fruit, sugar and treacle (molasses). Beat in the eggs and stout until the ingredients are well blended.

Turn into 4 well-greased 1.2 litre/2 pint/5 cup pudding basins (ovenproof bowls) to three-quarters full. Press down solidly to prevent air bubbles forming. Cover each basin with a double thickness of greaseproof (waxed) paper and foil, allowing a 2.5 cm/1 inch pleat in the centre to allow for expansion. Steam the puddings in pans of simmering water for 8 hours, then set aside to cool completely.
To freeze: remove from the basins and wrap in a double thickness of heavy-duty foil. Seal, label and freeze.
Storage life: up to 3 months
To thaw and serve: thaw overnight in the refrigerator. Return to the basins (bowls) and cover as before. Steam for 3 hours.
Makes 4 puddings

Chocolate ice cream

METRIC/IMPERIAL
300 ml/½ pint double
  cream
2 × 15 ml spoons/
  2 tablespoons milk
50 g/2 oz icing sugar,
  sifted
1 × 2.5 ml spoon/
  ½ teaspoon vanilla
  essence
2 × 15 ml spoons/
  2 tablespoons cocoa
  powder
4 × 15 ml spoons/4
  tablespoons boiling water

AMERICAN
1¼ cups heavy cream
2 tablespoons milk
½ cup confectioners' sugar,
  sifted
½ teaspoon vanilla extract
2 tablespoons unsweetened
  cocoa
¼ cup boiling water

Put the cream and milk into a bowl and beat until they form stiff peaks. Fold in the icing (confectioners') sugar and vanilla. Pour the mixture into an ice-cube tray or a shallow rigid container and freeze for 30 minutes, or until it begins to set around the edges. Blend the cocoa and water to a smooth paste. Transfer the setting ice cream to a bowl and beat in the cocoa paste until thoroughly blended. Return the mixture to the tray or container.
To freeze: cover, label and freeze.
Storage life: up to 2 months
To thaw and serve: thaw, covered, for 30 minutes in the refrigerator.
Serves 4

Blackcurrant sorbet

METRIC/IMPERIAL
0.5 kg/1 lb blackcurrants,
  frozen with sugar
100 g/4 oz sugar
300 ml/½ pint water
2 egg whites
lemon slices to decorate

AMERICAN
1 lb blackcurrants, frozen
  with sugar
½ cup sugar
1¼ cups water
2 egg whites
lemon slices to decorate

Thaw the fruit at room temperature for 3 to 4 hours. When soft, pour through a sieve (strainer) into a bowl. Put the sugar and water into a saucepan over a gentle heat and stir continuously until the sugar has dissolved. Increase the heat and boil, without stirring, for 8 minutes, or until the mixture is syrupy. Set aside to cool. Stir the syrup into the blackcurrant purée, then pour the mixture into an ice-cube tray or shallow rigid container. Put into the freezer for 1 hour, or until slightly mushy. Turn into a bowl and beat until smooth. Beat the egg whites until they form stiff peaks, then fold them into the blackcurrant mixture. Return to the tray or container.
To freeze: cover, label and return to the freezer.
Storage life: up to 3 months
To thaw and serve: thaw, covered, for 10 to 15 minutes in the refrigerator. Serve in individual glasses, decorated with a lemon slice.
Serves 6

Crêpes Suzette

Crêpes Suzette

METRIC/IMPERIAL
100 g/4 oz caster sugar
100 g/4 oz butter
finely grated rind of 1
   orange
juice of 2 large oranges
1 × 15 ml spoon/
   1 tablespoon cooking oil
1 × 15 ml spoon/
   1 tablespoon Grand
   Marnier
3 × 15 ml spoons/
   3 tablespoons brandy

Batter:
100 g/4 oz plain flour
pinch of salt
2 eggs
250 ml/8 fl oz milk
1 × 15 ml spoon/
   1 tablespoon melted
   butter

AMERICAN
½ cup superfine sugar
½ cup butter
finely grated rind of 1
   orange
juice of 2 large oranges
1 tablespoon cooking oil
1 tablespoon Grand
   Marnier
3 tablespoons brandy

Batter:
1 cup all-purpose flour
pinch of salt
2 eggs
1 cup milk
1 tablespoon melted butter

To make the batter, sift the flour and salt into a bowl. Make a well in the centre and add the eggs, then gradually beat in half the milk. Beat in the remaining milk and the melted butter. Set aside for 30 minutes.

Put the sugar, butter, orange rind and juice in a large frying pan and heat gently until the sugar has dissolved, stirring continuously. Simmer for 8 minutes, then set aside.

To make the crêpes, lightly brush the bottom of a medium frying pan with a little oil. Set over a moderate heat and pour over enough batter just to cover the base of the pan thinly. Cook until the underside is golden brown, turn over and cook the other side until golden brown. Slide the crêpe onto a wire rack to cool. Repeat, using the remaining oil to grease the pan between each crêpe.

Set the pan containing the sauce over a low heat and warm, stirring continuously. Put the crêpe into the sauce and fold into quarters. Transfer the folded crêpe to a rigid container. Repeat, using the remaining crêpes. Stir the Grand Marnier and brandy into the sauce remaining in the pan, then pour over the folded crêpes.

To freeze: cool quickly, cover, label and freeze.
Storage life: up to 3 months
To thaw and serve: put the frozen crêpes in a shallow ovenproof dish. Put, covered, into a pre-heated moderate oven (180°C/350°F, Gas Mark 4) for 20 minutes, separating the crêpes as they thaw.
Serves 4

Honey cream pie

METRIC/IMPERIAL
100 g/4 oz crushed
  digestive biscuits
50 g/2 oz butter, melted
25 g/1 oz brown sugar
1 × 2.5 ml spoon/
  ½ teaspoon ground
  cinnamon
1 × 175 g/6 oz can
  evaporated milk, chilled
finely grated rind and
  juice of 1 large lemon
1 × 15 ml spoon/
  1 tablespoon clear honey
15 g/½ oz powdered
  gelatine, dissolved in
  2 × 15 ml spoons/
  2 tablespoons boiling
  water

AMERICAN
1 cup crushed Graham
  crackers
¼ cup butter, melted
2½ tablespoons brown
  sugar
½ teaspoon ground
  cinnamon
1 × 6 oz can evaporated
  milk, chilled
finely grated rind and
  juice of 1 large lemon
1 tablespoon clear honey
1 tablespoon powdered
  gelatin, dissolved in
  2 tablespoons boiling
  water

Beat the crushed biscuits (crackers), butter, sugar and cinnamon together, then use to line the base of an 18 cm/7 inch loose-bottomed cake tin (pan). Chill in the refrigerator for 15 minutes.

Pour the evaporated milk into a bowl and beat until thick and creamy. Beat in the lemon rind and juice and honey. Strain the gelatine mixture into the honey mixture, beating continuously. Pour the mixture into the biscuit case (crumb crust).

To freeze: open freeze. When frozen, remove from the cake tin (pan), wrap in heavy-duty foil, seal, label and return to the freezer.

Storage life: up to 3 months

To thaw and serve: thaw, uncovered, for 1½ hours at room temperature.

Serves 4 to 6

Honey cream pie

Mocha delights

Mocha delights

METRIC/IMPERIAL	AMERICAN
6 eggs, separated	*6 eggs, separated*
25 g/1 oz butter	*2 tablespoons butter*
175 g/6 oz plain chocolate	*6 squares semi-sweet cooking chocolate*
2 × 15 ml spoons/ 2 tablespoons rum	*2 tablespoons rum*
3 × 15 ml spoons/ 3 tablespoons coffee essence	*3 tablespoons coffee flavoring*
120 ml/4 fl oz double cream to decorate	*½ cup heavy cream to decorate*

Put the egg yolks, butter and chocolate into a heat-proof bowl and set over a pan of simmering water. Heat over a low heat, stirring continuously until the chocolate has melted and the mixture is thick and smooth. Remove the bowl from the pan and beat in the rum and coffee essence (extract). Beat the egg whites until they form stiff peaks, then quickly fold into the coffee mixture. Pour into 8 small individual freezerproof pots or ramekins and set aside to cool and firm.

To freeze: open freeze. When frozen, cover tops with heavy-duty foil and put in a polythene (plastic) bag. Seal, label and return to the freezer.

Storage life: up to 3 months

To thaw and serve: thaw, uncovered, for 1 hour at room temperature. Beat the cream until thick and stiff, then pipe decoratively over each pot.

Serves 8

Mincemeat and apple pie

METRIC/IMPERIAL	AMERICAN
400 g/14 oz frozen shortcrust pastry, thawed	*14 oz frozen basic pie dough, thawed*
225 g/8 oz mincemeat	*1 cup mincemeat*
0.5 kg/1 lb cooking apples, peeled, cored, sliced and stewed	*1 lb baking apples, peeled, cored, sliced and stewed*
1 × 5 ml spoon/1 teaspoon grated orange rind	*1 teaspoon grated orange rind*
1 × 15 ml spoon/ 1 tablespoon milk	*1 tablespoon milk*

Divide the pastry dough in half. Roll out both halves on a lightly floured surface and use one half to line a 20 cm/8 inch foil pie dish (pan). Spoon in the mincemeat, then the apple slices and orange rind. Cover with the remaining dough piece, dampen the edges of the dough and crimp to seal. Cut a slit in the top of the dough to allow the steam to escape.

To freeze: open freeze. When frozen, cover with heavy-duty foil, seal, label and return to the freezer.

Storage life: up to 3 months

To thaw and serve: remove the cover and brush the top with the milk. Put into a preheated hot oven (220°C/425°F, Gas Mark 7) for 45 minutes, or until the pastry is golden brown.

Serves 4 to 6

Vanilla sauce

METRIC/IMPERIAL
25 g/1 oz cornflour
600 ml/1 pint milk or
  single cream
2 × 15 ml spoons/
  2 tablespoons caster
  sugar
1 × 5 ml spoon/1 teaspoon
  vanilla essence
15 g/½ oz butter

AMERICAN
¼ cup cornstarch
2½ cups milk or light
  cream
2 tablespoons superfine
  sugar
1 teaspoon vanilla extract
1 tablespoon butter

Mix the cornflour (cornstarch) and 3 × 15 ml spoons/ 3 tablespoons of milk or cream together to a smooth paste. Put the remaining milk or cream into a saucepan and heat slowly until it is very hot but not boiling. Stir in the cornflour (cornstarch) mixture until it is blended. Cook for 1 minute. Bring to the boil, stirring continuously, then simmer for 2 minutes. Remove from the heat and stir in the remaining ingredients.
To freeze: cool quickly and pour into a rigid container, in usable quantities. Cover, label and freeze.
Storage life: up to 3 months
To thaw and serve: turn into a saucepan and thaw over a very low heat. Heat until very hot, stirring continuously.
Makes 600 ml/1 pint/2½ cups

*Lemon syllabub

METRIC/IMPERIAL
1 large lemon
5 × 15 ml spoons/
  5 tablespoons medium
  sherry
1 × 15 ml spoon/
  1 tablespoon brandy
50 g/2 oz caster sugar
300 ml/½ pint double
  cream, stiffly beaten

AMERICAN
1 large lemon
⅓ cup medium sherry
1 tablespoon brandy
¼ cup superfine sugar
1¼ cups heavy cream,
  stiffly beaten

Grate the lemon rind into a mixing bowl, then squeeze over the juice. Stir in the sherry, brandy and sugar, stirring continuously, until the sugar has dissolved. Fold in the cream.
To freeze: turn into small individual rigid containers (yogurt or cream cartons) or a large rigid container. Cover, label and freeze.
Storage life: up to 3 months
To thaw and serve: dip the bottom of the container(s) into boiling water for 2 seconds, then invert onto a serving plate(s).
Serves 4

Melba sauce

METRIC/IMPERIAL
3 × 15 ml spoons/
  3 tablespoons redcurrant
  jelly
225 g/8 oz frozen
  raspberries
1 × 15 ml spoon/
  1 tablespoon hot water
50 g/2 oz sugar
1 × 15 ml spoon/
  1 tablespoon cornflour
1 × 15 ml spoon/
  1 tablespoon cold water
1 × 5 ml spoon/1 teaspoon
  lemon juice

AMERICAN
3 tablespoons redcurrant
  jelly
½ lb frozen raspberries
1 tablespoon hot water
¼ cup sugar
1 tablespoon cornstarch
1 tablespoon cold water
1 teaspoon lemon juice

Put the jelly, raspberries, hot water and sugar into a saucepan. Mix the cornflour (cornstarch) and cold water to a smooth paste, then stir into the sauce. Bring to the boil, then simmer for 2 minutes, stirring continuously. Remove from the heat, then rub through a fine sieve (strainer). Stir in the lemon juice.
To freeze: cool quickly and turn into a rigid container. Cover, label and freeze.
Storage life: up to 6 months
To thaw and serve: thaw for 2 to 3 hours at room temperature, then stir gently before serving.
Makes about 300 ml/½ pint/1¼ cups

Hard sauce

METRIC/IMPERIAL
100 g/4 oz butter
100 g/4 oz icing sugar,
  sifted
100 g/4 oz caster sugar
1 × 15 ml spoon/
  1 tablespoon single cream
2 × 15 ml spoons/
  2 tablespoons brandy
50 g/2 oz ground almonds
finely grated rind of 1
  orange

AMERICAN
½ cup butter
1 cup confectioners' sugar,
  sifted
½ cup superfine sugar
1 tablespoon light cream
2 tablespoons brandy
½ cup ground almonds
finely grated rind of 1
  orange

Beat the butter with a wooden spoon until it is soft and creamy. Gradually beat in the sugars, alternating them with the cream and brandy until the ingredients are well blended. Beat in the remaining ingredients.
To freeze: turn into a rigid container, cover, label and freeze.
Storage life: up to 3 months
To thaw and serve: thaw for 2 to 3 hours at room temperature. Stir gently before serving.
Serves 6

Oranges in Grand Marnier

Mixed fruit sauce

METRIC/IMPERIAL
*0.5 kg/1 lb mixed
uncooked fruit
4 × 15 ml spoons/
4 tablespoons water
100 g/4 oz caster sugar*

AMERICAN
*1 lb mixed uncooked fruit
4 tablespoons water
½ cup superfine sugar*

Put the fruit and water into a saucepan and simmer until the fruit is soft. Stir in the sugar until it has dissolved. Purée until smooth in a blender, then transfer to small rigid containers.
To freeze: cool quickly, cover, label and freeze.
Storage life: up to 9 months
To thaw and serve: thaw for 2 to 3 hours at room temperature.
Makes about 450 ml/¾ pint/2 cups

Oranges in Grand Marnier

METRIC/IMPERIAL
*8 large oranges
100 g/4 oz caster sugar
120 ml/4 fl oz Grand
Marnier*
To decorate:
*flaked almonds
grapes, deseeded*

AMERICAN
*8 large oranges
½ cup superfine sugar
½ cup Grand Marnier*
To decorate:
*slivered almonds
grapes, deseeded*

Finely grate the rind from 2 of the oranges. Peel all of the oranges, cut into thin slices and remove the pips (seeds). Arrange the slices in a large rigid container and sprinkle over the sugar and orange rind.
To freeze: cover, label and freeze.
Storage life: up to 9 months
To thaw and serve: thaw for 3 to 4 hours at room temperature. Transfer to a serving dish, sprinkle with the almonds and grapes and pour over the Grand Marnier.
Serves 8

Pineapple mousse

Pineapple mousse

METRIC/IMPERIAL	AMERICAN
3 eggs, separated	3 eggs, separated
juice of 1 lemon	juice of 1 lemon
50 g/2 oz caster sugar	¼ cup superfine sugar
15 g/½ oz powdered gelatine	2 × ¼ oz envelopes powdered gelatin
300 ml/½ pint pineapple juice	1¼ cups pineapple juice
150 ml/¼ pint double cream, stiffly beaten	⅔ cup heavy cream, stiffly beaten

Put the egg yolks, lemon juice and sugar into a heatproof bowl and set over a saucepan of simmering water. Heat over a low heat, beating continuously until the mixture is thick and pale. Remove the bowl from the pan and set aside to cool, beating occasionally.

Put the gelatine and about 3 × 15 ml spoons/ 3 tablespoons of the pineapple juice into a heatproof bowl set over a pan of simmering water. Heat over a low heat, stirring continuously until the gelatine has dissolved. Stir the mixture into the remaining pineapple juice, then fold the juice into the egg yolk mixture. Set aside in a cool place until it is on the point of setting, stirring frequently. Beat the egg whites until they form stiff peaks. Fold the egg whites into the setting pineapple mixture, with the cream.

To freeze: turn into a serving dish, cover and freeze. When frozen, dip the bottom of the dish into boiling water for 2 seconds, then invert the mousse onto a plate. Put in a polythene (plastic) bag, seal, label and return to the freezer.

Storage life: up to 3 months

To thaw and serve: return to the serving dish and thaw for 6 hours in the refrigerator.

Serves 6

Pineapple ice cream

METRIC/IMPERIAL	AMERICAN
1 medium pineapple, halved and cored	1 medium pineapple, halved and cored
juice of 1 large lemon	juice of 1 large lemon
175 g/6 oz sugar	¾ cup sugar
150 ml/¼ pint water	⅔ cup water
300 ml/½ pint double cream, lightly beaten	1¼ cups heavy cream, lightly beaten

Cut the pineapple flesh into chunks, reserving the juice and shells. Set the shells aside. Put the chunks, juice and lemon juice into a blender and purée until smooth. Transfer to a rigid container.

Put the sugar and water into a saucepan and bring slowly to the boil, stirring continuously until the sugar has dissolved. Set aside until the syrup has cooled and thickened slightly. Stir the syrup into the pineapple mixture.

To freeze: cool, cover and freeze until almost set. Turn into a bowl and beat briskly until broken up and light. Quickly fold in the cream and return to the container. Cover, label and freeze.

Storage life: up to 3 months

To thaw and serve: scoop out the ice cream with a scoop that has been dipped in hot water. Serve in the reserved pineapple shells.

Serves 6

Pineapple ice cream

Orange cheesecake

METRIC/IMPERIAL	AMERICAN
100 g/4 oz crushed digestive biscuits	1 cup crushed Graham crackers
50 g/2 oz butter, melted	¼ cup butter, melted
1 × 5 ml spoon/1 teaspoon ground allspice	1 teaspoon ground allspice
25 g/1 oz caster sugar	2 tablespoons superfine sugar

Filling:

225 g/8 oz cream cheese	1 cup cream cheese
1 × 175 g/6 oz can sweetened condensed milk	1 × 6 oz can sweetened condensed milk
grated rind and juice of 2 oranges	grated rind and juice of 2 oranges
150 ml/¼ pint double cream, lightly beaten	⅔ cup heavy cream, lightly beaten

Beat the crushed biscuits (crackers), butter, allspice and sugar together, then use to line a 20 cm/8 inch foil pie plate. Chill in the refrigerator for 15 minutes.

Combine all the filling ingredients together until they are thoroughly blended. Spoon the mixture into the biscuit base (crumb crust).

To freeze: cover loosely with heavy-duty foil and freeze until set and firm. Seal with a foil lid, put in a polythene (plastic) bag, seal, label and return to the freezer.

Storage life: up to 1 month

To thaw and serve: turn the pie out onto a serving plate and thaw for 1 hour at room temperature.

Serves 6

Iced raspberry soufflé

METRIC/IMPERIAL	AMERICAN
4 egg whites	4 egg whites
225 g/8 oz caster sugar	½ lb superfine sugar
0.5 kg/1 lb raspberries, puréed and sieved	1 lb raspberries, puréed and strained
300 ml/½ pint double cream, lightly whipped	1¼ cups heavy cream, lightly whipped
2 × 5 ml spoons/ 2 teaspoons brandy	2 teaspoons brandy

To decorate:

double cream, whipped	heavy cream, whipped
grated chocolate	grated chocolate

Beat the egg whites until they form stiff peaks, then beat in the sugar 1 × 15 ml spoon/1 tablespoon at a time. Fold in the raspberry purée, whipped cream and brandy. Pour the mixture into a freezerproof soufflé dish.

To freeze: open freeze, then wrap in heavy-duty foil. Seal, label and return to the freezer.

Storage life: up to 3 months

To thaw and serve: thaw, covered, for 1 hour in the refrigerator. Serve decorated with whipped cream and grated chocolate.

Serves 6

*Gooseberry fool

METRIC/IMPERIAL	AMERICAN
0.5 kg/1 lb gooseberries	1 lb gooseberries
100 g/4 oz sugar	½ cup sugar
4 × 15 ml spoons/	¼ cup water
4 tablespoons water	1¼ cups heavy cream
300 ml/½ pint double	
cream	

Put the gooseberries, sugar and water into a saucepan over a gentle heat and stir continuously until the sugar has dissolved. Cover and simmer until the gooseberries are tender. Pour the mixture through a sieve (strainer) into a bowl and set aside to cool. Beat the cream until it forms stiff peaks, then fold into the gooseberry mixture.

To freeze: turn into small individual rigid containers (yogurt or cream cartons), or a large rigid container. Cover, label and freeze.

Storage life: up to 3 months

To thaw and serve: thaw for 2 hours at room temperature and dip the bottom of the container(s) into boiling water for 2 seconds. Invert onto a plate and transfer to serving dishes. Serve with sponge fingers (ladyfingers).

Serves 4

Gooseberry fool

*Rhubarb and apple crumble

METRIC/IMPERIAL	AMERICAN
0.5 kg/1 lb rhubarb, chopped	1 lb rhubarb, chopped
0.5 kg/1 lb cooking apples, peeled, cored and chopped	1 lb baking apples, peeled, cored and chopped
175 g/6 oz brown sugar	1 cup brown sugar
grated rind and juice of 1 orange	grated rind and juice of 1 orange
Topping:	**Topping:**
225 g/8 oz plain flour	2 cups all-purpose flour
100 g/4 oz butter or margarine	½ cup butter or margarine
100 g/4 oz caster sugar	½ cup superfine sugar

Arrange the fruit in a freezerproof pie dish, then sprinkle over the sugar and orange rind and juice.

Sift the flour into a bowl, then rub in the butter or margarine until the mixture resembles fine breadcrumbs. Stir in the sugar. Sprinkle the topping mixture over the filling to enclose it completely.

To freeze: cover with heavy-duty foil, put in a polythene (plastic) bag, seal, label and freeze.

Storage life: up to 6 months

To thaw and serve: put, uncovered, into a preheated hot oven (220°C/425°F, Gas Mark 7) for 20 minutes. Reduce to moderately hot (190°C/375°F, Gas Mark 5) and bake for a further 45 minutes.

Serves 4 to 6

Tortoni

METRIC/IMPERIAL	AMERICAN
300 ml/½ pint double cream	1¼ cups heavy cream
300 ml/½ pint single cream	1¼ cups light cream
75 g/3 oz icing sugar, sifted	¾ cup confectioners' sugar, sifted
1 × 2.5 ml spoon/ ½ teaspoon vanilla essence	½ teaspoon vanilla extract
2 egg whites, stiffly beaten	2 egg whites, stiffly beaten
100 g/4 oz crushed macaroons	1 cup crushed macaroons
2 × 15 ml spoons/ 2 tablespoons medium sherry	2 tablespoons medium sherry

Pour the creams into a bowl and beat until they form stiff peaks. Stir in half the icing (confectioners') sugar and the vanilla. Fold the remaining icing (confectioners') sugar into the egg whites, then fold the mixture into the cream. Stir in the macaroons and sherry. Turn into 2 lightly oiled 600 ml/1 pint/2½ cup freezerproof moulds or foil-lined pudding basins (bowls).

To freeze: cover, label and freeze.

Storage life: up to 2 months

To thaw and serve: unwrap and remove from the moulds or basins (bowls). Thaw for 2½ hours in the refrigerator.

Each mould serves 4 to 6

Treacle tart

Treacle tart

METRIC/IMPERIAL
*175 g/6 oz frozen
   shortcrust pastry, thawed*
*250 ml/8 fl oz golden
   syrup*
*50 g/2 oz fresh white
   breadcrumbs*
*grated rind and juice of 1
   lemon*

AMERICAN
*6 oz frozen basic pie
   dough, thawed*
1 cup light corn syrup
*1 cup fresh white
   breadcrumbs*
*grated rind and juice of 1
   lemon*

Roll out the pastry dough on a lightly floured surface and use to line a well-greased 20 cm/8 inch flan dish (pie pan). Reserve the trimmings. Place the dish (pan) on a baking sheet.

Put the syrup, breadcrumbs and grated lemon rind and juice into a saucepan and heat gently until melted. Pour into the pastry case (pie shell). Roll out the trimmings and use to form a lattice pattern over the filling. Put the sheet into a preheated moderate oven (180°C/350°F, Gas Mark 4) and bake for 30 to 35 minutes, or until the pastry is golden brown.

To freeze: cool quickly, then open freeze. When frozen, wrap in heavy-duty foil, put in a polythene (plastic) bag, seal, label and return to the freezer.

Storage life: up to 6 months

To thaw and serve: thaw, uncovered, for 3 hours at room temperature. Serve cold, or put into a preheated moderate oven (180°C/350°F, Gas Mark 4) for 10 minutes.

Serves 4 to 6

107

Raspberry cheesecake

Raspberry cheesecake

METRIC/IMPERIAL
*175 g/6 oz crushed
  digestive biscuits
75 g/3 oz butter, melted
25 g/1 oz brown sugar
1 × 2.5 ml spoon/
  ½ teaspoon ground
  cinnamon*

Filling:
*1 packet lemon jelly
350 g/12 oz cream cheese
150 ml/¼ pint double
  cream
juice of 2 lemons
100 g/4 oz caster sugar
225 g/8 oz raspberries
4 × 15 ml spoons/
  4 tablespoons redcurrant
  jelly*

AMERICAN
*1½ cups crushed Graham
  crackers
6 tablespoons butter,
  melted
2½ tablespoons brown
  sugar
½ teaspoon ground
  cinnamon*

Filling:
*1 package lemon-
  flavored gelatin
1½ cups cream cheese
⅔ cup heavy cream
juice of 2 lemons
½ cup superfine sugar
½ lb raspberries
4 tablespoons redcurrant
  jelly*

To make the filling, dissolve the jelly (gelatin) in 150 ml/¼ pint/⅔ cup of boiling water. Stir in up to 300 ml/½ pint/1¼ cups of cold water and set aside until the jelly (gelatin) has thickened and is almost set.

Meanwhile, beat the crushed biscuits (crackers), butter, sugar and cinnamon together, then use to line the base of a 20 cm/8 inch loose-bottomed cake tin (pan). Chill in the refrigerator for 15 minutes.

Beat the cream cheese, cream, lemon juice and sugar together until they are blended, then gradually beat in the thickening jelly (gelatin). Spoon the mixture into the biscuit base (crumb crust).

To freeze: open freeze, then remove from the cake tin (pan), wrap in heavy-duty foil, seal, label and return to the freezer.

Storage life: up to 1 month

To thaw and serve: thaw overnight in the refrigerator. About 30 minutes before serving, arrange the raspberries in a circle around the edge of the filling. Melt the jelly, then spoon over the cheesecake.
Serves 6

Summer pudding

METRIC/IMPERIAL
*about 15 slices medium
    white bread*
*0.75 kg/1½ lb rhubarb,
    chopped*
0.5 kg/1 lb blackcurrants
225 g/8 oz blackberries
0.5 kg/1 lb sugar
150 ml/¼ pint water
0.5 kg/1 lb strawberries
225 g/8 oz raspberries
*600 ml/1 pint double
    cream, beaten*

AMERICAN
*about 15 slices medium
    white bread*
1½ lb rhubarb, chopped
1 lb blackcurrants
½ lb blackberries
2 cups sugar
⅔ cup water
1 lb strawberries
½ lb raspberries
*2½ cups heavy cream,
    beaten*

Cut 3 slices of bread to fit the top and 3 to fit the bottom, of 3 medium freezerproof pudding basins (bowls) or use freezerproof soufflé dishes. Cut the remaining bread into fingers. Put the bottom slices in place, then line the sides of the basins with bread fingers.

Put the rhubarb, blackcurrants, blackberries, sugar and water into a saucepan and bring slowly to the boil, stirring continuously until the sugar has dissolved. Simmer until the fruit are tender. Stir in the strawberries and raspberries and cook for 1 minute. Spoon the fruit into the lined basins, then cover with the reserved bread slices, to enclose the filling completely. Put a plate on top to weigh down and set aside to cool completely.

To freeze: remove the weight, cover, label and freeze.
Storage life: up to 6 months
To thaw and serve: thaw overnight in the refrigerator or for 8 hours at room temperature. Serve with the cream and any extra fruit.
Makes 3 puddings, each serving 4 people

Summer pudding

Fudge cake

METRIC/IMPERIAL
150 g/5 oz butter
400 g/14 oz caster sugar
2 eggs, beaten
1 × 5 ml spoon/1 teaspoon
  vanilla essence
75 g/3 oz plain chocolate,
  melted
50 g/2 oz walnuts, chopped
225 g/8 oz plain flour,
  sifted
1.5 × 5 ml spoons/
  1½ teaspoons baking
  powder
pinch of salt
300 ml/½ pint water
Icing:
50 g/2 oz butter
115 g/4½ oz icing sugar,
  sifted
1 × 15 ml spoon/
  1 tablespoon single
  cream

AMERICAN
½ cup plus 2 tablespoons
  butter
1¾ cups superfine sugar
2 eggs, beaten
1 teaspoon vanilla extract
3 squares semi-sweet
  cooking chocolate,
  melted
½ cup chopped walnuts
2 cups all-purpose flour,
  sifted
1½ teaspoons baking
  powder
pinch of salt
1¼ cups water
Icing:
¼ cup butter
1 cup confectioners' sugar,
  sifted
1 tablespoon light cream

Brownies

Cream the butter and sugar together until they are pale and fluffy. Beat in the eggs, one at a time, then the vanilla, melted chocolate and walnuts. Fold in the flour, baking powder and salt, alternating with the water. Spoon the batter into two 23 cm/9 inch sandwich tins (layer cake pans) lined with greased greaseproof (waxed) paper.

Put the tins (pans) into a preheated moderate oven (180°C/350°F, Gas Mark 4) and bake for 25 to 35 minutes, or until the cakes spring back when lightly pressed with a fingertip. Set aside in the tins (pans) for 5 minutes. Turn out of the tins (pans), remove the paper and transfer to a wire rack to cool completely.

Meanwhile, to make the icing, beat the butter with a wooden spoon until it is soft. Gradually beat in the icing (confectioners') sugar, alternating with the cream. The icing should be thick but fluffy. Cut the cakes in half, crosswise, and generously fill the layers with the icing. Sandwich the layers back together again to make one cake.

To freeze: open freeze. When frozen, put in a polythene (plastic) bag, seal, label and return to the freezer.

Storage life: up to 3 months

To thaw and serve: thaw for 3 to 4 hours at room temperature.
Serves 8

* Brownies

METRIC/IMPERIAL
75 g/3 oz plain chocolate,
  broken into pieces
100 g/4 oz butter
100 g/4 oz caster sugar
1 egg, beaten
1 × 5 ml spoon/1 teaspoon
  vanilla essence
150 g/5 oz plain flour
1 × 2.5 ml spoon/
  ½ teaspoon baking powder
pinch of salt
100 g/4 oz walnuts, finely
  chopped
milk

AMERICAN
3 squares semi-sweet
  cooking chocolate,
  broken into pieces
½ cup butter
½ cup superfine sugar
1 egg, beaten
1 teaspoon vanilla extract
1¼ cups all-purpose flour
½ teaspoon baking powder
pinch of salt
1 cup finely chopped
  walnuts
milk

Put the chocolate in a heatproof bowl and set over a pan of simmering water. Heat over a low heat, stirring continuously until the chocolate has melted. Remove the bowl from the pan. Cream the butter and sugar together until they are pale and fluffy, then beat in the egg and vanilla. Sift the flour, baking powder and salt into the mixture and beat well to blend. Fold in the melted chocolate and walnuts, with enough milk to give a thick, dropping consistency.

Spoon the mixture into a well-greased shallow 20 cm/8 inch square baking tin (pan) and put the tin (pan) into a preheated moderate oven (180°C/350°F, Gas Mark 4). Bake for 25 to 30 minutes, or until a knife inserted into the centre of the mixture comes out clean. Cut into squares and set aside in the tin to cool completely.

To freeze: remove from the tin and put in a polythene (plastic) bag. Seal, label and freeze.

Storage life: up to 6 months

To thaw and serve: thaw, uncovered, for 2 hours at room temperature.
Makes about 16

American flapjacks

METRIC/IMPERIAL	AMERICAN
100 g/4 oz butter	½ cup butter
100 g/4 oz brown sugar	⅔ cup brown sugar
5 × 15 ml spoons/ 5 tablespoons clear honey	⅓ cup clear honey
225 g/8 oz rolled oats	2 cups rolled or instant oats
2 × 5 ml spoons/ 2 teaspoons melted butter	2 teaspoons melted butter

Put the butter, sugar and honey into a saucepan and heat gently, stirring continuously until the butter has melted. Fold in the oats. Brush a Swiss roll tin (jelly roll pan) (about 20 cm × 30 cm/8 inches × 12 inches) with the melted butter, then turn the flapjack mixture into the tin (pan), spreading it out to cover evenly.

Put the tin (pan) into a preheated moderate oven (180°C/350°F, Gas Mark 4) and bake for 20 minutes, or until the mixture is golden brown. Set aside in the tin (pan) for 5 minutes, then cut into bars.

To freeze: cool quickly and turn into a rigid container, separating the layers with foil or greaseproof (waxed) paper. Cover, label and freeze.

Storage life: up to 6 months

To thaw and serve: thaw, uncovered, for 2 hours at room temperature.

Makes about 24

Butter crunch biscuits (cookies)

METRIC/IMPERIAL	AMERICAN
225 g/8 oz plain flour	2 cups all-purpose flour
pinch of salt	pinch of salt
175 g/6 oz butter	¾ cup butter
finely grated rind of ½ lemon	finely grated rind of ½ lemon
100 g/4 oz caster sugar	½ cup superfine sugar
25 g/1 oz sugar	2 tablespoons sugar

Sift the flour and salt into a bowl. Beat the butter with a wooden spoon until it is soft. Beat in the lemon rind and caster (superfine) sugar until the mixture is pale and fluffy. Fold in the flour and remaining sugar. Divide the dough into 2 equal portions. Roll out on a lightly sugared surface to form 2 sausage shapes, about 15 cm/6 inches long. Wrap in foil and chill in the refrigerator until they are firm.

To freeze: cut each roll into about 16 slices and put on a baking sheet. Open freeze. When frozen, put in rigid containers, separating each layer with foil or greaseproof (waxed) paper. Cover, label and return to the freezer.

Storage life: up to 6 months

To thaw and serve: transfer the frozen biscuits (cookies) to greased baking sheets and put into a preheated moderate oven (160°C/325°F, Gas Mark 3) for 40 minutes, or until they are pale golden around the edges.

Makes about 32

Bakewell tart

METRIC/IMPERIAL	AMERICAN
175 g/6 oz frozen shortcrust pastry, thawed	6 oz frozen basic pie dough, thawed
100 g/4 oz butter	½ cup butter
100 g/4 oz caster sugar	½ cup superfine sugar
100 g/4 oz ground almonds	1 cup ground almonds
1 egg	1 egg
1 × 2.5 ml spoon/ ½ teaspoon almond essence	½ teaspoon almond extract
2 × 15 ml spoons/ 2 tablespoons raspberry jam	2 tablespoons raspberry jam

Roll out the pastry dough on a lightly floured surface and use to line a 20 cm/8 inch flan dish (pie pan). Reserve the trimmings. Put the dish on a baking sheet.

Melt the butter in a saucepan and stir in the sugar. Heat gently for 1 minute, stirring continuously until the sugar has dissolved. Stir in the ground almonds, egg and almond essence (extract). Set aside to cool slightly.

Spread the jam over the bottom of the pastry case (pie shell), then spoon over the filling. Roll out the trimmings and use them to make a lattice pattern over the filling. Put the sheet into a preheated moderately hot oven (200°C/400°F, Gas Mark 6) and bake for 25 minutes, or until the filling is set and the pastry is golden brown.

To freeze: cool quickly, then open freeze. When frozen, wrap in heavy-duty foil and put in a polythene (plastic) bag. Seal, label and return to the freezer.

Storage life: up to 6 months

To thaw and serve: thaw for 6 hours at room temperature, then put into a preheated moderate oven (180°C/350°F, Gas Mark 4) for 25 minutes.

Serves 4 to 6

Cob loaf

METRIC/IMPERIAL	AMERICAN
0.5 kg/1 lb risen basic white dough (see page 112)	4 cups basic risen white dough (see page 112)

Shape the dough into a deep round. Put into a well-greased 15 cm/6 inch cake tin (pan). Cover and put into a warm place for about 45 minutes, or until the dough comes up to the top of the tin (pan).

Put the tin (pan) into a preheated moderately hot oven (200°C/400°F, Gas Mark 6) and bake for 40 minutes, or until the bread is risen and golden brown. Set aside to cool. Remove from the tin (pan).

To freeze: put in a polythene (plastic) bag or wrap in heavy-duty foil. Seal, label and freeze.

Storage life: up to 2 months

To thaw and serve: thaw, covered, for 3 to 4 hours at room temperature. Or put, covered, into a preheated moderately hot oven (200°C/400°F, Gas Mark 6) for 45 minutes.

Makes 1 loaf

*Basic white bread dough

METRIC/IMPERIAL	AMERICAN
1 × 5 ml spoon/1 teaspoon sugar	1 teaspoon sugar
40 g/1½ oz fresh yeast	1½ cakes compressed yeast
900 ml/1½ pints tepid milk	3¾ cups tepid milk
1.5 kg/3 lb plain flour	12 cups all-purpose flour
1 × 15 ml spoon/ 1 tablespoon salt	1 tablespoon salt
100 g/4 oz butter or margarine, cut into small pieces	½ cup butter or margarine, cut into small pieces

Put the sugar and yeast into a large bowl. Add the milk and blend until smooth.

Sift the flour and salt into another large bowl. Add the butter or margarine and rub into the flour until the mixture resembles fine breadcrumbs. Add the yeast liquid and beat until the dough is smooth and comes away from the sides of the bowl.

Turn out onto a lightly floured surface and knead for about 10 minutes, or until the dough is smooth and elastic. Lightly grease the bowl, shape the dough into a ball and return to it. Cover and set aside in a warm place for 45 minutes to 1 hour, or until the dough has doubled in size. Turn out onto a lightly floured surface and knead again for 5 minutes, or until it is smooth and firm.

To freeze: form into a cylindrical shape and put in a lightly oiled polythene (plastic) bag. Seal, label and freeze.

Storage life: up to 3 weeks

To thaw: unseal the polythene (plastic) bag, then retie loosely at the top. Thaw overnight in the refrigerator or for 4 to 6 hours at room temperature. The dough is now ready for shaping, proving and baking.

Makes 1.5 kg/3 lb

Chocolate biscuits (cookies)

METRIC/IMPERIAL	AMERICAN
100 g/4 oz margarine	½ cup margarine
100 g/4 oz caster sugar	½ cup superfine sugar
1 small egg, beaten	1 small egg, beaten
few drops vanilla essence	few drops vanilla extract
225 g/8 oz plain flour	2 cups all-purpose flour
25 g/1 oz cocoa powder	¼ cup unsweetened cocoa
50 g/2 oz flaked chocolate	2 oz flaked chocolate
175 g/6 oz plain chocolate, broken into pieces and melted	6 squares semi-sweet cooking chocolate, broken into pieces and melted

Cream the margarine and sugar together until they are pale and light, then beat in the egg and vanilla. Sift the flour and cocoa into the mixture, then stir in the flaked chocolate. Beat well, then turn onto a lightly floured surface and knead to a smooth dough. Wrap in a polythene (plastic) bag and chill in the refrigerator for 20 minutes.

Roll out the dough to about 5 mm/¼ inch thick, then, using a pastry (cookie) cutter, cut into 5 cm/ 2 inch rounds. Remove the centres with smaller cutters and transfer the rounds to greased baking sheets. Put the sheets into a preheated moderately hot oven (190°C/375°F, Gas Mark 5) and bake for 15 minutes. Set aside on the sheets for 5 minutes, then transfer to a wire rack to cool completely. Dip the top of each ring into the melted chocolate and set aside to set on oiled greaseproof (waxed) paper.

To freeze: when set, turn into rigid containers, using foil or greaseproof (waxed) paper to separate the layers. Cover, label and freeze.

Storage life: up to 6 months

To thaw and serve: unwrap and thaw for 1 hour at room temperature.

Makes about 24

Coffee gâteau

METRIC/IMPERIAL	AMERICAN
225 g/8 oz butter	1 cup butter
225 g/8 oz caster sugar	1 cup superfine sugar
4 small eggs, beaten	4 small eggs, beaten
225 g/8 oz self-raising flour, sifted	2 cups self-rising flour, sifted
2 × 15 ml spoons/ 2 tablespoons coffee essence	2 tablespoons coffee flavoring
75 g/3 oz walnuts, chopped	¾ cup chopped walnuts
whole walnuts to decorate	whole walnuts to decorate
Icing:	**Icing:**
100 g/4 oz butter	½ cup butter
225 g/8 oz icing sugar, sifted	2 cups confectioners' sugar, sifted
2 × 15 ml spoons/ 2 tablespoons single cream	2 tablespoons light cream

Cream the butter and sugar together until they are pale and fluffy. Beat in the eggs, one at a time, adding 1 × 15 ml spoon/1 tablespoon of flour with each one. Fold in the remaining flour, with the coffee essence (extract) and walnuts, and beat well until blended. Spoon the batter into a 20 cm/8 inch cake tin (pan) lined with greased greaseproof (waxed) paper. Put the tin into a preheated moderate oven (180°C/350°F, Gas Mark 4) and bake for 40 to 50 minutes, or until the cake springs back when lightly pressed with a fingertip. Set aside in the tin (pan) for 5 minutes, remove the paper and transfer to a wire rack to cool completely.

Meanwhile, to make the icing, beat the butter with a wooden spoon until it is soft. Gradually beat in the icing (confectioners') sugar, alternating with the cream. The icing should be thick but fluffy. Coat the top and sides of the cake generously with the icing.

To freeze: open freeze. When frozen put in a polythene (plastic) bag, seal, label and return to the freezer.

Storage life: up to 3 months

To thaw and serve: thaw, uncovered, for 3 to 4 hours at room temperature. Serve decorated with whole walnuts.

Serves 8

Iced tea ring; Poppy seed twist (page 120); Fruit loaf (page 115)

Iced tea ring

METRIC/IMPERIAL
*350 g/12 oz risen basic
  white dough (see page
  112)*
15 g/½ oz butter, melted
50 g/2 oz brown sugar
*1 × 5 ml spoon/1 teaspoon
  ground cinnamon*
25 g/1 oz almonds, chopped
Icing:
*50 g/2 oz icing sugar,
  sifted*
*1 × 5 ml spoon/1 teaspoon
  tepid water*
To decorate:
*1.5 × 15 ml spoons/
  1½ tablespoons flaked
  toasted almonds
glacé cherries*

AMERICAN
*3 cups risen basic white
  dough (see page 112)*
1 tablespoon butter, melted
⅓ cup brown sugar
*1 teaspoon ground
  cinnamon*
¼ cup chopped almonds

Icing:
*½ cup confectioners' sugar,
  sifted*
1 teaspoon tepid water

To decorate:
*1½ tablespoons slivered
  toasted almonds
candied cherries*

Roll out the pastry dough on a lightly floured surface to a rectangle about 30 cm × 23 cm/12 inches × 9 inches. Brush with melted butter, then sprinkle over the sugar, cinnamon and almonds. Roll up firmly and seal the edges. Bring the ends together to form a ring, sealing the ends, and transfer to a greased baking sheet. Using scissors, make cuts about 2.5 cm/1 inch apart to within 1 cm/½ inch of the centre. Separate by turning each piece sideways a little. Cover and put into a warm place for 45 minutes, or until the ring has risen. Put the sheet into a preheated moderately hot oven (200°C/400°F, Gas Mark 6) and bake for 30 minutes. Set aside to cool completely.

Meanwhile, to make the icing, beat the icing (confectioners') sugar and water together to make a smooth paste. Dribble the icing over the bread ring, then scatter over the almonds and cherries. Set aside until set.

To freeze: put in a polythene (plastic) bag, seal, label and freeze.

Storage life: up to 2 months

To thaw and serve: thaw, covered, for 3 to 4 hours at room temperature.

Serves 10 to 12

113

Gingerbread

Gingerbread

METRIC/IMPERIAL	AMERICAN
150 ml/¼ pint milk	⅔ cup milk
1 × 5 ml spoon/1 teaspoon bicarbonate of soda	1 teaspoon baking soda
100 g/4 oz butter	½ cup butter
120 ml/4 fl oz golden syrup	½ cup light corn syrup
120 ml/4 fl oz treacle	½ cup molasses
75 g/3 oz brown sugar	½ cup brown sugar
1 × 15 ml spoon/ 1 tablespoon orange marmalade	1 tablespoon orange marmalade
100 g/4 oz self-raising flour, sifted	1 cup self-rising flour, sifted
100 g/4 oz wholemeal flour	1 cup wholewheat flour
1 × 5 ml spoon/1 teaspoon ground allspice	1 teaspoon ground allspice
2 × 15 ml spoons/ 2 tablespoons ground ginger	2 tablespoons ground ginger
salt	salt
2 eggs, beaten	2 eggs, beaten
25 g/1 oz blanched almonds, flaked	3 tablespoons blanched slivered almonds

Put the milk and soda into a saucepan and warm until it is tepid. Set aside. Put the butter, syrup, treacle (molasses), sugar and marmalade into a second saucepan and heat until the butter has melted, stirring continuously. Put the flours, spices and salt into a bowl, then stir in the treacle (molasses) mixture, milk and eggs, and beat to a smooth batter.

Spoon the mixture into a 20 cm/8 inch cake tin (pan) lined with greased greaseproof (waxed) paper, sprinkle with the almonds, and put into a preheated moderate oven (160°C/325°F, Gas Mark 3). Bake for 1 hour, or until a knife inserted into the centre of the cake comes out clean. Set aside to cool in the tin (pan), then turn out and remove the paper.

To freeze: wrap in heavy-duty foil, seal, label and freeze.

Storage life: up to 3 months

To thaw and serve: thaw for 3 hours at room temperature.

Serves 8 to 10

Jalousie

METRIC/IMPERIAL	AMERICAN
0.5 kg/1 lb cooking apples, peeled, cored and sliced	1 lb baking apples, peeled, cored and sliced
2 × 15 ml spoons/ 2 tablespoons water	2 tablespoons water
25 g/1 oz butter	2 tablespoons butter
50 g/2 oz sugar	¼ cup sugar
400 g/14 oz frozen puff pastry, thawed	14 oz frozen puff pastry, thawed
1 egg white, lightly beaten	1 egg white, lightly beaten

Put the apples, water, butter and sugar into a saucepan. Cover and simmer until the apples are tender. Uncover and simmer until most of the liquid has evaporated. Mash with a fork or purée until smooth in a blender. Set aside to cool.

Roll out the pastry dough on a lightly floured surface, to a rectangle about 20 cm × 30 cm/8 inches × 12 inches. Divide the dough in half, lengthways, and transfer one half to a greased baking sheet. Spoon the apple purée over the dough, leaving a 1 cm/½ inch margin at the edges. Fold the remaining dough in half lengthways, then cut across the fold at about 5 cm/ 2 inch intervals. Leave a 2.5 cm/1 inch margin at the edges. Unfold the dough and arrange on top of the filling. Dampen the edges of the dough, then crimp to seal.

To freeze: open freeze. When frozen, wrap in heavy-duty foil, seal, label and return to the freezer.

Storage life: up to 3 months

To thaw and serve: brush the egg white over the top of the dough. Put into a preheated moderately hot oven (200°C/400°F, Gas Mark 6) for 35 to 40 minutes, or until the pastry is puffed up and golden brown. Serve hot or cold.

Serves 6 to 8

Garlic bread

Garlic bread

METRIC/IMPERIAL
1 French loaf
225 g/8 oz butter,
softened
3 garlic cloves, crushed
1.5 × 5 ml spoons/
1½ teaspoons dried mixed
herbs

AMERICAN
1 French loaf
1 cup butter, softened
3 garlic cloves, crushed
1½ teaspoons dried mixed
herbs

Make cuts to within about 5 mm/¼ inch of the base (bottom) of the loaf, at about 2.5 cm/1 inch intervals. Beat all the remaining ingredients together until blended, then spread generously between the slices.
To freeze: wrap in heavy-duty foil and put in a polythene (plastic) bag. Seal, label and freeze.
Storage life: up to 2 weeks
To thaw and serve: put foil-wrapped into a pre-heated moderate oven (180°C/350°F, Gas Mark 4) for 15 minutes. Uncover and raise the heat to hot (230°C/450°F, Gas Mark 8) for 10 minutes. Serve hot.

Fruit cake

METRIC/IMPERIAL
200 g/7 oz self-raising
flour
pinch of salt
100 g/4 oz glacé cherries,
halved
150 g/5 oz butter
115 g/4½ oz caster sugar
2 large eggs, beaten
2 × 15 ml spoons/
2 tablespoons brandy
1 × 0.5 kg/1 lb can
pineapple chunks,
drained and finely
chopped
350 g/12 oz mixed dried
fruit (sultanas,
currants, etc.)

AMERICAN
1¾ cups self-rising flour
pinch of salt
½ cup candied cherries,
halved
½ cup plus 2 tablespoons
butter
½ cup plus 1 tablespoon
superfine sugar
2 large eggs, beaten
2 tablespoons brandy
1 × 1 lb can pineapple
chunks, drained and
finely chopped
2 cups mixed dried fruit
(seedless white raisins,
currants, etc.)

Sift the flour and salt together. Put about three-quarters of the cherries in a little flour to prevent them from sinking to the bottom of the cake. Chop the remaining cherries into small pieces and reserve. Cream the butter and sugar together until they are pale and light. Beat in the eggs, adding a tablespoon of flour with each one. Fold in the remaining flour with the brandy and all the remaining ingredients, except the chopped cherries. Blend well, then turn into a 1.5 kg/3 lb loaf tin (pan) lined with greased grease-proof (waxed) paper. Scatter the reserved cherry pieces on top.
   Put the tin into a preheated moderate oven (160°C/325°F, Gas Mark 3) and bake for 2 hours, or until a knife inserted into the centre comes out clean. Set aside to cool, then turn out and remove the paper.
To freeze: wrap in foil, seal, label and freeze.
Storage life: up to 3 months
To thaw and serve: thaw for 4 to 5 hours at room temperature.
Serves 10 to 12

Fruit loaf

METRIC/IMPERIAL
0.5 kg/1 lb risen basic
white dough (see page
112)
50 g/2 oz sultanas
25 g/1 oz candied peel,
chopped
grated rind of 1 lemon

AMERICAN
4 cups basic risen white
dough (see page 112)
⅓ cup seedless white
raisins
3 tablespoons chopped
candied peel
grated rind of 1 lemon

Work together all the ingredients. Shape the dough into an oblong, the same width as a 0.5 kg/1 lb loaf tin (pan). Fold in three and turn over so the seam is underneath. Smooth over the top and place in a greased loaf tin (pan). Place in a large, oiled polythene (plastic) bag and leave to rise until the dough doubles in size or rises to the top of the tin (pan). Bake in a preheated moderately hot oven (200°C/400°F, Gas Mark 6) for 30 to 35 minutes. Remove from the tin (pan) and set aside to cool.
To freeze: put in a polythene (plastic) bag, or wrap in heavy-duty foil. Seal, label and freeze.
Storage life: up to 2 months
To thaw and serve: thaw, covered, for 4 to 5 hours at room temperature.
Makes 1 loaf

Mince pies

Lemon Swiss (jelly) roll

METRIC/IMPERIAL	AMERICAN
3 large eggs, at room temperature	3 large eggs, at room temperature
75 g/3 oz caster sugar	6 tablespoons superfine sugar
75 g/3 oz self-raising flour, sifted	¾ cup self-rising flour, sifted
100 g/4 oz lemon curd (see page 34)	¼ lb lemon curd (see page 34)

Put the eggs and sugar into a bowl and beat until they are frothy. Fold in the flour and beat well. Spoon the mixture into a Swiss roll tin (jelly roll pan) (about 30 cm × 23 cm/12 inches × 9 inches) lined with greased greaseproof (waxed) paper. Put the tin (pan) into a preheated moderately hot oven (190°C/375°F, Gas Mark 5) and bake for 15 to 20 minutes, or until the cake is firm to the touch. Turn out onto greaseproof (waxed) paper sprinkled with sugar. Trim the edges to make a neat rectangle, then spread over the lemon curd. Carefully roll up the mixture. Set aside on a wire rack to cool.

To freeze: open freeze. When frozen, wrap in heavy-duty foil, seal, label and return to the freezer.

Storage life: up to 4 months

To thaw and serve: loosen the wrapping and thaw for 3 to 4 hours at room temperature.

Serves 6

Mince pies

METRIC/IMPERIAL	AMERICAN
0.5 kg/1 lb self-raising flour	4 cups self-rising flour
225 g/8 oz butter, cut into small pieces	1 cup butter, cut into small pieces
50 g/2 oz lard, cut into small pieces	¼ cup lard, cut into small pieces
1 egg, separated	1 egg, separated
milk	milk
0.75 kg/1½ lb mincemeat	1½ lb mincemeat
caster sugar	superfine sugar
icing sugar to decorate	confectioners' sugar to decorate

Sift the flour into a bowl. Add the fats and rub them into the flour until the mixture resembles fine breadcrumbs. Beat in the egg yolk, with enough milk to make a firm dough. Knead until the dough is well blended, then chill in the refrigerator for 15 minutes.

Roll out the pastry dough on a lightly floured surface. Using a 7.5 cm/3 inch pastry (cookie) cutter, cut out about 32 rounds and use them to line greased tartlet tins (patty pans). Roll out the remaining dough and, using a 5 cm/2 inch pastry (cookie) cutter, cut out the same number of rounds for lids. If liked, cut out a star shape in the centre of each lid. Fill the tartlet tins (patty shells) with the mincemeat. Dampen the edges of the dough, fit on the lids and crimp to seal.

Beat the egg white until it is frothy, then brush over the tops of the dough. Dust with caster (superfine) sugar. Put the tins (pans) into a preheated moderately hot oven (200°C/400°F, Gas Mark 6) and bake for 20 minutes, or until the pastry is golden brown.

To freeze: cool quickly, then open freeze in the tins (pans). When frozen, turn out of the tins (pans) and put in polythene (plastic) bags. Seal, label and return to the freezer.

Storage life: up to 3 months

To thaw and serve: return to the tins (pans) and put into a preheated moderately hot oven (200°C/400°F, Gas Mark 6) for 25 minutes. Serve sprinkled with icing (confectioners') sugar.

Makes 32

Malt loaf

METRIC/IMPERIAL	AMERICAN
175 g/6 oz self-raising flour	1½ cups self-rising flour
2 × 15 ml spoons/ 2 tablespoons malt drink	2 tablespoons malt drink
25 g/1 oz caster sugar	2 tablespoons superfine sugar
75 g/3 oz dried mixed fruit (sultanas, currants, etc.)	½ cup dried mixed fruit (seedless white raisins, currants, etc.)
2 × 15 ml spoons/ 2 tablespoons golden syrup	2 tablespoons light corn syrup
150 ml/¼ pint milk	⅔ cup milk

Put all the ingredients into a large bowl and beat until they are well blended. Spoon the mixture into a well-greased 0.5 kg/1 lb loaf tin (pan) and put into a preheated moderate oven (180°C/350°F, Gas Mark 4). Bake for 1 hour, or until a knife inserted into the centre of the loaf comes out clean. Transfer to a wire rack to cool.

To freeze: wrap in heavy-duty foil, seal, label and freeze.

Storage life: up to 3 months

To thaw and serve: thaw for 4 hours at room temperature.

Serves 6 to 8

Savarin

METRIC/IMPERIAL

1 × 5 ml spoon/1 teaspoon
  sugar
25 g/1 oz fresh yeast
175 ml/6 fl oz tepid milk
175 g/6 oz plain flour,
  sifted
pinch of salt
75 g/3 oz butter, melted
3 eggs, lightly beaten
1 × 5 ml spoon/1 teaspoon
  caster sugar
Syrup:
100 g/4 oz sugar
300 ml/½ pint water
juice of 1 large lemon
3 × 15 ml spoons/
  3 tablespoons rum

AMERICAN

1 teaspoon sugar
1 cake compressed yeast
¾ cup tepid milk
1½ cups all-purpose flour,
  sifted
pinch of salt
6 tablespoons butter,
  melted
3 eggs, lightly beaten
1 teaspoon superfine
  sugar
Syrup:
½ cup sugar
1¼ cups water
juice of 1 large lemon
3 tablespoons rum

Put the sugar and yeast into a small bowl. Add the milk and blend until smooth.

Sift the flour and salt together into a bowl. Make a well in the centre and pour in the yeast mixture, butter, eggs and sugar and beat well. Pour the mixture into a well-greased 20 cm/8 inch savarin or ovenproof ring mould (tube pan). Cover and set aside in a warm place for 45 minutes or until the dough has risen to the top of the mould.

Put the mould (pan) into a preheated hot oven (220°C/425°F, Gas Mark 7) and bake for 20 minutes. Reduce the heat to moderately hot (190°C/375°F, Gas Mark 5) and bake for a further 15 minutes, or until the savarin is golden brown. Set aside in the mould (pan) to cool completely.

To freeze: turn out of the mould (pan) and wrap in heavy-duty foil. Seal, label and freeze.

Storage life: up to 1 month

To thaw and serve: thaw, covered, overnight in the refrigerator. Uncover and transfer to a deep serving dish. Prick all over with a fork.

To make the syrup, put the sugar, water and lemon juice in a saucepan over a gentle heat and stir continuously until the sugar has dissolved. Bring to the boil, and cook for 5 minutes, stirring occasionally, or until the syrup thickens. Stir in the rum. Pour the syrup over the savarin and set aside to soak for 10 minutes. Fill the centre with fresh fruit before serving. Serves 8

Savarin

Profiteroles

Profiteroles

METRIC/IMPERIAL
Choux pastry:
150 g/5 oz plain flour
pinch of salt
75 g/3 oz butter
300 ml/½ pint water
4 eggs, well beaten
Filling and sauce:
300 ml/½ pint double
* cream, stiffly beaten*
175 g/6 oz plain chocolate,
* broken into pieces*
100 g/4 oz caster sugar
1 × 15 ml spoon/
* 1 tablespoon cocoa*
* powder*
450 ml/¾ pint water
2 egg yolks

AMERICAN
Choux pastry:
1¼ cups all-purpose flour
pinch of salt
6 tablespoons butter
1¼ cups water
4 eggs, well beaten
Filling and sauce:
1¼ cups heavy cream,
* stiffly beaten*
6 squares semi-sweet
* cooking chocolate,*
* broken into pieces*
½ cup superfine sugar
1 tablespoon
* unsweetened cocoa*
2 cups water
2 egg yolks

Sift the flour and salt into a bowl. Put the butter and water into a saucepan and heat gently, stirring continuously until the butter has melted. Bring to the boil, then remove from the heat. Quickly fold in the flour and return to the heat. Cook, stirring continuously, until the mixture is smooth and begins to come away from the sides of the pan. Cool slightly, then beat in the eggs, a little at a time, until the mixture is smooth and shiny. Remove from the heat and set aside to cool.

Spoon the mixture into a piping (pastry) bag with a plain nozzle, and pipe the mixture in small balls onto greased baking sheets. Put the sheets into a preheated moderately hot oven (200°C/400°F, Gas Mark 6) and bake for 15 to 20 minutes, or until they are well risen and golden brown. Make a slit in the side of each puff to let the steam escape and return to the oven for a further 5 minutes to dry out. Set aside on a wire rack to cool completely.

To freeze: put in a polythene (plastic) bag, seal, label and freeze.

Storage life: up to 6 months

To thaw and serve: thaw, covered, for 1 hour at room temperature, then put into a preheated moderate oven (180°C/350°F, Gas Mark 4) for 5 minutes. Set aside to cool completely. Fill with the whipped cream and pile onto a serving dish.

Put the chocolate, sugar, cocoa and water in a saucepan and heat gently, stirring continuously, until the chocolate melts. Simmer for 15 minutes, stirring occasionally. Set aside to cool a little, then beat in the egg yolks. Set aside to cool, then pour the sauce over the profiteroles.
Makes about 35

Moravian fruit cake

METRIC/IMPERIAL	AMERICAN
225 g/8 oz butter	1 cup butter
225 g/8 oz caster sugar	1 cup superfine sugar
4 eggs, beaten	4 eggs, beaten
100 g/4 oz glacé pineapple, chopped	⅔ cup chopped candied pineapple
100 g/4 oz glacé cherries, chopped	⅔ cup chopped candied cherries
225 g/8 oz plain flour, sifted	2 cups all-purpose flour, sifted
1 × 5 ml spoon/1 teaspoon baking powder	1 teaspoon baking powder
2 × 15 ml spoons/ 2 tablespoons chopped walnuts	2 tablespoons chopped walnuts
50 g/2 oz ground almonds	⅓ cup ground almonds
Icing:	**Icing:**
175 g/6 oz butter	¾ cup butter
350 g/12 oz icing sugar, sifted	2⅔ cups confectioners' sugar, sifted
juice and grated rind of 2 lemons	juice and grated rind of 2 lemons

Cream the butter and sugar together until pale and fluffy. Add the eggs, one at a time, beating well between each addition. Stir in the glacé (candied) fruit, then fold in the flour and baking powder. Add the walnuts and almonds and beat until the ingredients are well blended.

Spoon the mixture into a 20 cm/8 inch cake tin (pan) lined with greased greaseproof (waxed) paper. Put the tin (pan) into a preheated moderate oven (180°C/350°F, Gas Mark 4) and bake for 1¼ hours, or until the cake springs back when lightly pressed with a finger-tip. Set aside in the tin (pan) for 5 minutes, remove the paper and transfer to a wire rack to cool completely.

Meanwhile, to make the icing, beat the butter with a wooden spoon until it is soft. Gradually beat in the icing (confectioners') sugar, alternating with the lemon juice and rind. The icing should be thick but fluffy. Coat the top and sides of the cake generously with the icing, bringing it up into decorative patterns with the flat edge of a knife.

To freeze: open freeze. When frozen, wrap in heavy-duty foil, seal, label and return to the freezer.

Storage life: up to 3 months

To thaw and serve: thaw, uncovered, for 3 hours at room temperature.

Serves 8 to 10

Moravian fruit cake

119

Poppy seed twist

METRIC/IMPERIAL	AMERICAN
350 g/12 oz risen basic white dough (see page 112)	3 cups risen basic white dough (see page 112)
1 egg	1 egg
1 × 5 ml spoon/1 teaspoon sugar	1 teaspoon sugar
1 × 15 ml spoon/ 1 tablespoon water	1 tablespoon water
2 × 15 ml spoons/ 2 tablespoons poppy seeds	2 tablespoons poppy seeds

Divide the dough into 2 equal pieces and roll out each between the palms of your hands until they are about 30 cm/12 inches long. Pinch one end of each length together, then plait loosely, pinching the other ends together when you reach them. Transfer the bread to a greased baking sheet, cover and put in a warm place for 30 to 40 minutes, or until the bread spreads across the sheet.

Meanwhile, beat the egg, sugar and water together. Brush the mixture over the risen dough and sprinkle over the poppy seeds. Put the sheet into a preheated moderately hot oven (200°C/400°F, Gas Mark 6) and bake for 30 minutes, or until the bread is risen and golden brown. Set aside to cool.

To freeze: put in a polythene (plastic) bag, or wrap in heavy-duty foil. Seal, label and freeze.

Storage life: up to 2 months

To thaw and serve: thaw, covered, for 3 to 4 hours at room temperature. Or put, covered, into a preheated moderately hot oven (200°C/400°F, Gas Mark 6) for 45 minutes.

Makes 1 loaf

Rich shortbread

METRIC/IMPERIAL	AMERICAN
225 g/8 oz butter	1 cup butter
100 g/4 oz caster sugar	½ cup superfine sugar
275 g/10 oz plain flour	2½ cups all-purpose flour
50 g/2 oz rice flour	½ cup rice flour

Cream the butter and sugar together until they are pale and fluffy. Sift the flours together, then gradually beat into the butter mixture. Knead the mixture gently until it is smooth. Shape the mixture into 2 rounds, about 18 cm/7 inches in diameter, and arrange them on a well-greased baking sheet. Prick the tops all over with a fork and mark out triangular serving portions with a knife. Chill in the refrigerator for 20 minutes.

Put the sheet into a preheated moderate oven (160°C/325°F, Gas Mark 3) and bake for 30 minutes, or until the shortbread is pale golden brown. Set aside on the sheet for 5 minutes, then cut into triangles while still soft. Transfer to a wire rack to cool completely.

To freeze: wrap in heavy-duty foil, seal, label and freeze.

Storage life: up to 3 months

To thaw and serve: thaw, uncovered, for 2 to 3 hours at room temperature.

Makes about 16

Rich chocolate cake

METRIC/IMPERIAL	AMERICAN
300 g/11 oz caster sugar	1⅓ cups superfine sugar
5 × 15 ml spoons/ 5 tablespoons water	⅓ cup water
75 g/3 oz cocoa powder	¾ cup unsweetened cocoa
175 ml/6 fl oz milk	¾ cup milk
225 g/8 oz butter	1 cup butter
4 eggs, separated	4 eggs, separated
225 g/8 oz self-raising flour, sifted	2 cups self-rising flour, sifted
2 × 5 ml spoons/ 2 teaspoons baking powder	2 teaspoons baking powder
150 ml/¼ pint double cream	⅔ cup heavy cream
150 ml/¼ pint single cream	⅔ cup light cream

Put 75 g/3 oz/6 tablespoons of sugar, the water and cocoa in a saucepan and mix to a smooth paste. Heat over a low heat, stirring continuously until the mixture is smooth and shiny. Stir in the milk and set aside to cool. Cream the butter and remaining sugar together until they are pale and fluffy, then beat in the egg yolks and chocolate mixture. Gradually fold in the flour and baking powder. Beat the egg whites until they form stiff peaks, then fold into the cake mixture.

Put the mixture into two 20 cm/8 inch sandwich tins (layer cake pans) lined with greased greaseproof (waxed) paper. Put the tins (pans) into a preheated moderate oven (180°C/350°F, Gas Mark 4) and bake for 40 minutes, or until the cakes spring back when lightly pressed with a fingertip.

Turn the cakes out of the tins (pans), remove the paper and set aside to cool on a wire rack. Beat the creams together until they form stiff peaks. Cut each cake in half, crosswise and generously fill the layers with cream. Sandwich the layers back again into one cake.

To freeze: wrap in heavy-duty foil, seal, label and freeze.

Storage life: up to 3 months

To thaw and serve: thaw for 5 hours at room temperature.

Serves 8

Rich chocolate cake

*Scones

METRIC/IMPERIAL	AMERICAN
0.5 kg/1 lb self-raising flour	4 cups self-rising flour
1 × 5 ml spoon/1 teaspoon salt	1 teaspoon salt
100 g/4 oz butter or margarine, cut into small pieces	½ cup butter or margarine, cut into small pieces
100 g/4 oz sugar	½ cup sugar
300 ml/½ pint milk or buttermilk	1¼ cups milk or buttermilk

Sift the flour and salt into a bowl. Add the butter or margarine and rub into the flour until the mixture resembles fine breadcrumbs. Stir in the sugar and enough milk to make a soft dough.

Turn the dough out onto a lightly floured surface and roll out to about 1 cm/½ inch thick. Using a 5 cm/2 inch pastry (cookie) cutter, cut the dough into rounds. Transfer to a lightly floured baking sheet and put into a preheated hot oven (220°C/425°F, Gas Mark 7). Bake for 12 to 15 minutes, or until the scones are lightly browned. Transfer to a wire rack to cool completely.

To freeze: put in a polythene (plastic) bag, seal, label and freeze.

Storage life: up to 6 months

To thaw and serve: put into a preheated moderate oven (180°C/350°F, Gas Mark 4) for 20 minutes. Serve warm.

Makes about 18 to 20

Scotch pancakes

METRIC/IMPERIAL	AMERICAN
225 g/8 oz plain flour	2 cups all-purpose flour
pinch of salt	pinch of salt
1 × 5 ml spoon/1 teaspoon bicarbonate of soda	1 teaspoon baking soda
1.5 × 5 ml spoons/ 1½ teaspoons cream of tartar	1½ teaspoons cream of tartar
1 egg	1 egg
milk	milk
corn oil	corn oil

Sift the flour, salt, soda and cream of tartar into a bowl. Make a well in the centre and pour in the egg and enough milk to give a smooth, thick batter (it should be the consistency of thick cream).

Lightly brush a heavy frying pan (skillet) or griddle with a little oil and put over a moderate heat. Drop 15 ml spoonfuls/tablespoonfuls of the batter, 2 or 3 at a time, onto the pan and cook until the surface bubbles. Turn over and cook on the other side until set. Transfer to a warm tea (dish) towel to keep moist while you cook the remaining batter in the same way.

To freeze: cool quickly and pack into rigid containers, separating the layers with foil or greaseproof (waxed) paper. Cover, label and freeze.

Storage life: up to 6 months

To thaw and serve: thaw, uncovered, for 1 hour at room temperature.

Makes about 35

Scones

Scottish shortbread

Walnut bread

METRIC/IMPERIAL	AMERICAN
0.5 kg/1 lb plain flour	*4 cups all-purpose flour*
4 × 5 ml spoons/	*4 teaspoons baking*
* 4 teaspoons baking*	* powder*
* powder*	*1 cup superfine sugar*
225 g/8 oz caster sugar	*1 cup chopped walnuts*
100 g/4 oz walnuts,	*1½ cups light corn syrup*
* chopped*	*1 cup milk*
350 ml/12 fl oz golden	*2 eggs, lightly beaten*
* syrup*	
250 ml/8 fl oz milk	
2 eggs, lightly beaten	

Sift the flour and baking powder into a mixing bowl
and stir in the sugar and walnuts. Put the syrup and
milk into a saucepan and heat gently until the syrup
has melted. Make a well in the centre of the flour
mixture and pour in the syrup mixture, with the eggs.
Beat until the ingredients are well blended, then
transfer to two 1 kg/2 lb loaf tins (pans) lined with
greased greaseproof (waxed) paper. Put the tins (pans)
into a preheated moderate oven (160°C/325°F, Gas
Mark 3) and bake for 1¼ hours, or until the loaves
spring back when lightly pressed with a fingertip. Set
aside to cool.
To freeze: put in a polythene (plastic) bag, seal, label
and freeze.
Storage life: up to 3 months
To thaw and serve: thaw overnight at room
temperature.
Makes 2 loaves

Scottish shortbread

METRIC/IMPERIAL	AMERICAN
100 g/4 oz plain flour	*1 cup all-purpose flour*
50 g/2 oz cornflour	*½ cup cornstarch*
100 g/4 oz butter	*½ cup butter*
50 g/2 oz caster sugar	*¼ cup superfine sugar*
2 × 15 ml spoons/	*2 tablespoons extra*
* 2 tablespoons extra*	* superfine sugar*
* caster sugar*	

Sift the flour and cornflour (cornstarch) into a bowl.
Cream the butter with a wooden spoon until it is soft,
then beat in the 50 g/2 oz/¼ cup of sugar. Beat in the
flours, 1 × 15 ml spoon/1 tablespoon at a time. Shape
the mixture into a firm dough and press out into a
well-greased 18 cm × 28 cm/7 inch × 11 inch Swiss roll
tin (jelly roll pan). Prick the top all over with a fork,
then lightly mark out into bars with a knife. Chill in
the refrigerator for 20 minutes.
　Put the tin (pan) into a preheated moderate oven
(160°C/325°F, Gas Mark 3) and bake for 30 to 35
minutes, or until the shortbread is pale golden brown.
Set aside in the tin (pan) for 5 minutes, then cut into
bars while still soft. Transfer to a wire rack to cool
completely.
To freeze: wrap in heavy-duty foil, seal, label and
freeze.
Storage life: up to 3 months
To thaw and serve: thaw, uncovered, for 2 to 3
hours at room temperature. Sprinkle over the extra
sugar before serving.
Makes about 8

Special fruit cake

Special fruit cake

METRIC/IMPERIAL	AMERICAN
225 g/8 oz self-raising flour	2 cups self-rising flour
1 × 2.5 ml spoon/ ½ teaspoon salt	½ teaspoon salt
50 g/2 oz glacé cherries, quartered	¼ cup quartered candied cherries
175 g/6 oz butter, softened	¾ cup butter, softened
175 g/6 oz brown sugar	1 cup brown sugar
3 eggs	3 eggs
2 × 15 ml spoons/ 2 tablespoons milk	2 tablespoons milk
225 g/8 oz sultanas	1⅓ cups seedless white raisins
175 g/6 oz raisins	1 cup raisins
1 × 15 ml spoon/ 1 tablespoon golden syrup	1 tablespoon light corn syrup
25 g/1 oz demerara sugar	2 tablespoons brown sugar

Sift the flour and salt into a bowl. Add all the remaining ingredients, except the demerara (brown) sugar, and beat well together. Spoon into a 1 kg/2 lb loaf tin (pan) lined with greased greaseproof (waxed) paper and sprinkle over the demerara (light brown) sugar.

Put the tin (pan) into a preheated cool oven (150°C/300°F, Gas Mark 2) and bake for 2 hours, or until a knife inserted into the centre of the cake comes out clean. Set aside in the tin (pan) for 10 minutes, remove the paper and transfer to a wire rack to cool completely.

To freeze: wrap in heavy-duty foil, seal, label and freeze.

Storage life: up to 3 months

To thaw and serve: thaw, uncovered, for 4 hours at room temperature.

Serves 12 to 15

Wheatmeal bread

METRIC/IMPERIAL	AMERICAN
1 × 15 ml spoon/ 1 tablespoon sugar	1 tablespoon sugar
25 g/1 oz fresh yeast	1 cake compressed yeast
450 ml/¾ pint tepid water	2 cups tepid water
350 g/12 oz strong plain white flour, sifted	3 cups all-purpose flour, sifted
350 g/12 oz wholemeal flour	3 cups wholewheat flour
2 × 5 ml spoons/ 2 teaspoons salt	2 teaspoons salt
1 × 15 ml spoon/ 1 tablespoon vegetable oil	1 tablespoon vegetable oil
2 × 15 ml spoons/ 2 tablespoons cracked wheat	2 tablespoons cracked wheat

Put the sugar and yeast into a large bowl. Add the water and blend until smooth. Sift the two flours and salt into another large bowl. Make a well in the centre and pour in the yeast mixture and oil, and beat until the dough is smooth and comes away from the sides of the bowl. Turn out onto a lightly floured surface and knead for about 10 minutes, or until the dough is smooth and elastic.

Lightly grease the bowl. Shape the dough into a ball and return it to the bowl. Cover and set aside in a warm place for 1 hour, or until the dough has doubled. Turn out onto the lightly floured surface and knead again for 5 minutes, or until it is smooth and firm. Divide the dough in half and shape either into rounds or rectangular shapes, depending on the containers in which you will cook them. Put the shapes into well-greased 12.5 cm/5 inch diameter clay flowerpots or 0.5 kg/1 lb loaf tins (pans). Cover and put in a warm place for 30 minutes, or until the dough has risen to the tops of the containers. Brush the loaves with a little salted water and sprinkle with the cracked wheat. Put the containers into a preheated hot oven (230°C/450°F, Gas Mark 8) and bake for 30 to 40 minutes, or until the loaves are risen and golden brown. Set aside to cool.

To freeze: put in a polythene (plastic) bag or wrap in heavy-duty foil. Seal, label and freeze.

Storage life: up to 2 months

To thaw and serve: thaw, covered, for 3 to 4 hours at room temperature. Or put, covered, into a preheated moderately hot oven (200°C/400°F, Gas Mark 6) for 45 minutes.

Makes 2 loaves

Wheatmeal bread

INDEX

Acknowledgments

The publishers would like to thank the following individuals and organizations for their kind permission to reproduce the photographs in this book.

Argentine Beef Bureau 35; Bryce Attwell endpapers, 2/3, 122; Carrier Cookshop 51; Crocks Reject China 36; Flour Advisory Bureau 71, 83, 99, 113, 118; Melvin Grey 19, 21, 25, 27, 49, 55, 62, 66, 70, 72, 77, 84, 87, 89, 91, 93, 101, 104, 108, 109, 110, 114, 115, 121, 125; Paul Kemp 29, 30, 32, 34, 38, 41, 42, 45, 52, 86, 92, 96, 97, 100, 106, 107, 119, 124; Lawrys Foods Inc. 69; Michael Leale 59; David Levin 4/5; John Lee 46, 47, 61, 94; Mazola 116; New Zealand Lamb Information Bureau 75; Roger Phillips 81; R.H.M. Foods Ltd. 98; Syndication International 39, 78, 117; Jerry Tan, Electricity Council Photographic Unit 6, 7, 9, 12/13, 37, 57, 63, 65, 105, 123.